HELPING CHILDREN COPE WITH THE DEATH OF A PARENT

Helping Children Cope with the Death of a Parent

A Guide for the First Year

Paddy Greenwall Lewis and Jessica G. Lippman

Contemporary Psychology
Chris E. Stout, Series Editor

Westport, Connecticut
London

Library of Congress Cataloging-in-Publication Data

Lewis, Paddy Greenwall, 1945–
Helping children cope with the death of a parent : a guide for the first year /
Paddy Greenwall Lewis and Jessica G. Lippman.
    p. cm.—(Contemporary psychology, ISSN 1546–668X)
   Includes bibliographical references and index.

   1. Bereavement in children. 2. Parents—Death—Psychological aspects. I.
Lippman, Jessica G., 1941– II. Title. III. Contemporary psychology (Praeger
Publishers)
BF723.G75L49 2004
155.9'37'083—dc22   2003053669

British Library Cataloguing in Publication Data is available.

Library of Congress Catalog Card Number: 2003053669

ISBN: 978-0-313-36155-5
ISSN: 1546–668X

First published in 2004

Praeger Publishers, 88 Post Road West, Westport, CT 06881
An imprint of Greenwood Publishing Group, Inc.
www.praeger.com

Printed in the United States of America

The paper used in this book complies with the
Permanent Paper Standard issued by the National
Information Standards Organization (Z39.48–1984).

10 9 8 7 6 5 4 3 2 1

We wish to dedicate this book to the memory of
Sylvia Hofman Greenwall

CONTENTS

Series Foreword

As this new millennium dawns, humankind has evolved—some would argue has devolved—exhibiting new and old behaviors that fascinate, infuriate, delight, or fully perplex those of us seeking answers to the question, "Why?" In this series, experts from various disciplines peer through the lens of psychology telling us answers they see for questions of human behavior. Their topics may range from humanity's psychological ills—addictions, abuse, suicide, murder, and terrorism among them—to works focused on positive subjects including intelligence, creativity, athleticism, and resilience. Regardless of the topic, the goal of this series remains constant—to offer innovative ideas, provocative considerations, and useful beginnings to better understand human behavior.

Series Editor
Chris E. Stout, Psy.D., MBA
Northwestern University Medical School
Illinois Chief of Psychological Services

Advisory Board

Bruce E. Bonecutter, Ph.D.
University of Illinois at Chicago
Director, Behavioral Services, Elgin Community Mental Health Center

Joseph A. Flaherty, M.D.
University of Illinois College of Medicine and College of Public Health
Chief of Psychiatry, University of Illinois Hospital

PREFACE

In our years of private practice we have treated many children who have lost mothers or fathers. The stories we have heard from these children demonstrate the profound loss and pain that the death of a parent causes.

With the publication of *Motherless Daughters*, we started a therapy group for motherless daughters. It shortly became apparent that there was no other such group in the metropolitan Chicago area. One group, meeting once a week for two years, became two groups, two groups became three. The knowledge and insight we acquired was staggering. These young women articulated and validated all that we had heard from our child patients and from our academic studies in psychology. These young women taught and illuminated for us what would have helped *them* as children; painstakingly, they revealed how their hurt was confounded by well-meaning, but psychologically un-aware, fathers, teachers, friends, and relatives. We heard over and over again:

"My father was a good man, a decent man, but he didn't know what to do. He was clueless. The message was not to talk about Mom. He thought he was protecting us from the pain by not reminding us of her. He hoped we would forget or get over it and somehow every-thing would be OK."

It was shortly after this time that a young friend and colleague of ours became ill. Her struggle with cancer and her legacy to her children (then ages 9 and 7) moved us deeply and personally. We felt that we needed to do more. More for her children, more for all children who experienced this pain, and more for the clueless and helpless fathers or mothers and other well-meaning, but insensitive, adults.

Enter Josh. Josh came for a consultation and stayed for two years. An extremely well-educated businessman, Josh was referred for consultation by an oncologist after his wife was diagnosed with pancreatic cancer. Josh and his wife, a nationally known lawyer, had a wide array of contacts all over the country who supplied them with readings on the latest research, the best medications, and the cutting edge in technology. Together they spent endless hours on the Internet and in medical libraries pursuing the most up-to-date information. But there was little available to help them deal with the emotional needs and reactions of their 10-year-old son and 3-year-old daughter. They could find no book that could sequentially guide them, no book that could offer practical information, or help them identify and address the psychological needs of their children when dealing with the loss of their mother.

Over the next 18 months, we helped Josh and his children deal with the mother's failing health, her frequent hospitalizations, her death, and the emotional devastation of the year that followed her death. We counseled them on the way to handle certain situations, certain events, and the children's reactions to all types of circumstances on a week-by-week basis. As the year unfolded, the trauma these motherless children were facing was illustrated over and over again. And although the grandparents and aunts and uncles were supportive, loving, and well-meaning, they often would offer advice or suggestions that were counterproductive and psychologically misguided.

It was during this time that we decided that it was imperative that parents, like Josh, have access to a practical guide that would take them step-by-step through the issues their children would face in the first year after a mother's or father's death. We also realized that such a guide would also benefit other caring adults such as extended family members, caregivers, teachers, clergy, and counselors.

Drawing on our many years of clinical experience, our work with individual patients, our specialization in children, and our Motherless Daughter groups, we started to write such a guide. Throughout the guide Josh's children, Arthur and Shelly, appear over and over again, as we follow them through the first devastating year without their mother.

In the same way that the Bible uses parables to teach valuable lessons, we have incorporated the memories, thoughts, and stories of those who have suffered the loss of a parent in childhood. It is our hope that this technique will be helpful to those who are raising a motherless or fatherless child.

ACKNOWLEDGMENTS

We wish to thank all those who have contributed to this book, but particularly Peter S. Lewis, Professor Matthew Lippman, Amelia Barrett, Julie Walski, our typist Judi Hannigan, and our editor Debbie Carvalko.

We would like to especially thank the Silverman sisters, Jane, Julia, and Maggie, for their rich and moving contribution to this book.

Without our patients, this book could never have been written. We would like to acknowledge them and honor the memory of their parents. We find it noteworthy that many patients chose the name of their deceased parent as their pseudonym. We hope that by including the names, memories, and stories of their loved ones we have provided a little additional comfort to them.

Acknowledgments

We wish to thank all those who have contributed to this book, but particularly Peter S. Lewis, Professor Matthew Lippman, Amelia Barrett, Julie Walski, our typist Judi Hannigan, and our editor Debbie Carvalko.

We would like to especially thank the Silverman sisters, Jane, Julia, and Maggie, for their rich and moving contribution to this book.

Without our patients, this book could never have been written. We would like to acknowledge them and honor the memory of their parents. We find it noteworthy that many patients chose the name of their deceased parent as their pseudonym. We hope that by including the names, memories, and stories of their loved ones we have provided a little additional comfort to them.

CHAPTER 1

ENDINGS

Anticipation of the Death: Saying Good-bye

All of us thrive when our lives are ordered, when we can anticipate events and prepare for them. The unexpected is seldom welcome. For a child, stability and structure are particularly essential for a feeling of well-being. When children's routines are disrupted, their fragile coping mechanisms can shatter. Serious disruptions such as severe illness, divorce, or death can leave them unable to navigate the labyrinth of sorrow, anxiety, confusion, and sadness. Their stability vanishes.[1]

> Jack was ten years old when his father died. He had not been told that his father was ill. That summer he happily went off to summer camp with no anticipation or preparation for what was to come. "I guess I should have realized that something was not right when they didn't show up for parents week-end, but they sent my older brothers and that seemed great. . . . It was only when I returned home at the end of the summer that I found out my father had died. They didn't tell me anything . . . there was no warning, nothing. I ran into the house shouting 'Dad, Dad!' Then they told me. It took me years and years to overcome the resulting anxiety, the need to control everything—I was quite the perfectionist (!)—and to finally trust significant people in my life."

It is not always possible to prepare for the unexpected. It is not always possible to prepare a child for the unforeseen. It is not always possible to anticipate and prepare a child for the death of a parent.

However, when a parent is very ill and death is expected, preparing the child for that death is essential. As part of the preparation, the healthy parent needs to speak with the child frequently during and about the illness. The well parent also needs to speak about the child's feelings surrounding the illness, the changes in the family's schedule, and life in general.

Developmentally, young children do not understand the concept of death, although by the age of 3, children have the capacity to miss someone. Maria Nagy (1948, 1959)[2] identifies three stages of childhood mourning. During the first stage—from ages 3 to 5—children see death as a departure, with the deceased now existing somewhere else.[3] Before the age of 6, children do not understand death and its finality. In Nagy's second stage—from ages 6 to 9—children personify death and believe that it can sometimes be avoided. From the age of 6 to age 12, children feel profound loss, yet their emotions have not reached a level of mastery. Nagy states that at the third stage, ages 9 to 12, children understand that death is inevitable and affects all people, including themselves.

Children need clear and honest information about their parents' illnesses, and it should be given at a level they can understand. These conversations should take place soon after a terminal diagnosis has been made. Children will be less anxious if they are kept informed. Depending on the age of the child each conversation will be different. For example, with a young child under the age of seven, one might say, "Daddy went to the doctor today. The doctor said Daddy is very sick. The doctor is going to try to make Daddy better, but he may not be able to." In this way the child has been introduced to the idea that the father is gravely ill. With an older child, over the age of seven, one might say, "Dad got some very bad news today. The tests came back and the doctor said he will need surgery/chemotherapy/radiation. It's very serious, and we hope he gets better. This is going to be a tough time. Things at home are going to be different. Dad may not be able to work for a while, and I will have more responsibility, so everybody will have to help in different ways."

When an illness requires hospitalization, it is important to begin preparing a child to visit the sick parent in the hospital. Hospitals can be frightening, overwhelming places particularly for young children. There are strange smells, dimly lit corridors, frightening medical apparatus, beds with bars, and strange, unfamiliar mechanical sounds. A parent's appearance may also be altered which may be upsetting. The parent can look physically paler, thinner, strained, and less alert.

The parent can also be depressed and therefore less talkative, less animated, less available, and less interested in what is going on in the child's world. The parent can appear detached and listless. The healthy parent needs to prepare the child for all of this prior to the hospital visit. The healthy parent needs to describe the hospital building, the entrance to the hospital, and the things the child may see on the way to the sick parent's room. The room should be described: what the bed looks like, the medical equipment that surrounds the parent, including the intravenous containers, heart monitors, and any other unfamiliar objects. In preparing a child for the ill parent's altered physical appearance, the healthy parent may say something such as, "Daddy's medicine has made him much thinner."

As the illness progresses, it is important for the healthy parent to begin talking with the child about the illness's severity. It is beneficial for the healthy parent to alert the child to the seriousness of the illness, the pain and the discomfort that the other parent is suffering, and the concern of the doctors and hospital staff. In this way the parent begins to prepare the child for the eventuality of the death. These conversations should be unrushed and should take place in comfortable, familiar, secure surroundings. Ideally, they should occur with no distractions, during unhurried times, allowing for questions, discussion, thinking time, and time to return to the painful subject. Such conversations should not be sandwiched between piano lessons and soccer, for example. Weekends are often the best time for these discussions, because much time can be given to talking and soothing.

The information can be not only preoccupying, but potentially paralyzing. For this reason the conversation should not take place at night. Children need plenty of time to return with questions rather than be traumatized with fear and possible nightmares. They need time to deal with upsetting information during waking hours. It is important to allow them a long period of time to digest distressing information.

These conversations allow a child time to digest the information and slowly learn to anticipate the fact that death will occur. A parent should begin to prepare the child with phrases such as, "Remember, I told you I didn't know if Mom would be coming home? The doctors are now saying that Mom is very, very sick, and they think she won't live much longer." The healthy parent should not be reluctant to show his or her own sadness. It is helpful to the child to know, by example, that sorrow is permissible. The expression of feeling is important. Stoicism and bravery are not to be encouraged. Extreme grief, however, should not be shared with the child.

A child might ask many questions. Simple answers are the most preferable. If euphemisms are used, the child may later feel betrayed and mistrustful.

> At 17 Bruce was an angry adolescent. His mother felt she had had little control over him since he was 9. In therapy, Bruce revealed that he felt he could never trust his mother following his father's death. His father had died when he was 8 years old. When his mother returned from the hospital on the day his father died, Bruce asked his mother how his father was doing. She replied, "Dad's resting." Bruce, satisfied at the answer, went out to play. Later that night he heard his mother crying and talking on the phone about his father's death. "I felt so betrayed, she never told me."

> Lonnie, an African-American young man, was six years old when his father died: "They never let me see him in the hospital. They said he 'passed.' I was happy. I thought he passed a test. I was going through the house happy and jumping. I was so happy he was coming home. He had been in the hospital a few weeks. I did not see him. I saw people in the house. An older cousin said, 'Why are you happy? He is never coming home.' I got angry with my cousin and got into a fight with her and asked my aunt if what she said was true. My aunt said, 'Yes, he died.'"

Family dynamics and a dying parent's awareness and acceptance of his or her impending death will determine whether there are final good-byes. There are instances when a parent, in preparation for death, writes a letter to the children, writes stories for them about their lives together, and even draws illustrations of family events for them. This is a marvelous gift to leave to the children. It is, however, only appropriate when it is instigated by the parent, when the parent has the physical and emotional strength to do this, and when the parent has accepted the finality of his or her own death.

At the time of death, the surviving parent needs to inform a child of the mother's or father's death in as gentle a manner as possible. A parent should hold a very young child on his or her lap when telling the child that their mother or father has died. It may be helpful to have a transitional object on hand, such as a favorite teddy bear or blanket. The parent should break the news gradually. For example, "I have something very sad to tell you. It's going to make you very sad, and Teddy very sad. You know that Mommy was very, very sick, but now she doesn't have to suffer anymore. She died a little while ago." Ideally, the parent should be as available as possible following this conversation. A child should never be left alone following the news of the death of the mother or father, although an adolescent may prefer some time alone. Regardless, there should be an available adult in the house.

> Steven, an active, curious nine year old, participated in multiple after-school activities. He was so busy that he was hardly aware that his mother was dying. He knew she was sick, and he had visited her once or twice during the early stages of her hospitalization. However, both his parents had presented an upbeat façade and had not talked with him about the seriousness of his mother's illness nor prepared him for her death. He awoke one morning to the sound of his father's sobs. Disturbed, he went into his father's study, and asked, "What's the matter?" Abruptly his father said, "Your mother died early this morning." The child, totally unprepared, was devastated. Years later, Steven's wife was hospitalized for a fairly mild condition and he found himself inexplicably and profoundly depressed. He was referred for therapy, where he recounted the story of his mother's "sudden death." Had Steven been at all prepared for the death of his mother, he would not have had this severe reaction 30 years later.

> "We did not discuss mother's death. I never brought it up to Dad, and he never brought it up to me. Afterwards, I kept thinking, 'What will I do when I don't have a mother anymore? What will I do?'" (Mary, age 15).

During this difficult time, surviving parents are propelled into the new role of single parent. At the very time that they are trying to cope with their own grief, they must respond to their children's needs as well. Yet, to ensure the children's future healthy adjustment, surviving parents have to pay attention to their own emotions as well as those of their children. Parents should not use their children as sounding boards or therapists, overwhelming roles for which no child is prepared. Rather surviving parents should turn to family members, friends, or counselors for support.

Preparing a Child for the Funeral

> "The only thing I remember about my father's funeral is my mother starting to fall and me catching her. I was only six years old. I don't remember ever crying for my dad. All I remember is wiping away my mother's tears. We would sit on the couch, she would cry and cry. I would sit there with the box of tissues wiping her tears, trying to cheer her up, and consoling her. It's no wonder I have a drug problem, huh?"

Visitations and funerals are very difficult times. According to William Worden, "Children who are not prepared for the funeral were more likely to show disturbed behavior, and low self-esteem, two years after the death of the parent."[4] Children need to be told ahead of time exactly what to expect at the visitation and funeral: How they will get to the funeral, who they will sit with at the funeral, what will happen at the service, where the casket will be, what will happen at the gravesite, who will be with them after the funeral, and how they will get home. It is strongly advised that young children not view the body in an open casket as this could be both frightening and upsetting.

> "I remember running around the grave in my prettiest party dress. It had little pink roses on it, and I wore my ruffly socks with my black patent Mary Jane's," so said Susan, with tears in her eyes, 20 years after her mother's funeral. "It was all so confusing, no one told me what was going on. There were lots of people. I'm not sure I even knew my mother was dead." Susan went on to describe how she remembered waking up in the middle of the night after the funeral in a strange bed, frightened, and missing her mother and father. At the age of 25, Susan still has difficulties coping with feelings of abandonment, the unpredictability of relationships, and the overriding issue of trust.

Sometimes, it is wise for children to attend only the religious service and not attend the actual graveside burial. This decision needs to be made on an individual basis, depending on a particular child and his or her psychological make-up. Potentially, the actual burial could be very upsetting. This is a very personal decision and needs to be carefully made. Young, vulnerable, and sensitive children should not attend the burial. If it is decided that it is inadvisable for a particular child to attend the burial, arrangements should then be made with someone, such as the mother of a close friend or a familiar baby-sitter, to be with the child when everyone else is at the cemetery. After the burial and condolence ritual, it is important that the surviving parent return home and spend the entire evening and night with the children. They need the presence of the remaining parent to help them feel secure.

The Child's Immediate Reaction

> "The night my father died I woke up terrified from a nightmare that he was calling to me from across a river, and I couldn't reach him. I was 10 years old. I screamed for my mom and realized that I was all alone in the apartment. I later found out she and my younger brother were at my grandmother's, downstairs. For years afterwards I had trouble falling asleep. I guess I was afraid of being alone." (Winnie, age 16).

Initially, children respond to death with a variety of reactions: sadness, crying, anxiety, and sleeplessness. Following a parent's long protracted illness, there is sometimes a sense of relief that the deceased is no longer suffering. Some children may not wish to talk much, seem untroubled by and appear indifferent to the parent's death. They may prefer to watch their favorite television programs, play outside with their friends, proceed with planned activities, and act as if nothing has happened. This does not mean that they don't miss or mourn the deceased parent. Nor does this response foretell future reactions, which could be very different.

Vicky, age 12, seemed indifferent to her mother's death. Her mother had died the day before Halloween after an illness that had lasted several years. She insisted on going trick-or-treating with her friends. She seemed cavalier and displayed no grief, interested only in the costume she was wearing and rigid in her determination to continue with her plans. The adults close to her were confused and perplexed by this reaction to her mother's death. A wise aunt brought her for therapy. Only after many months of therapy was she able to focus on her profound depression at the loss of her mother.

"I was a zombie that first year. I had nobody. No one could handle the way I was acting." (Diane, age 14).

An adolescent's emotions are well illustrated by Pauline, age 13. "Died on Thursday, buried on Sunday, school on Monday. I don't remember very much of high school. I would stay up all night and watch TV. I'd come home and eat junk food."

Tessa was 15 when her mother died. "I came home from school. My mother wanted to go back to the hospital. She wanted morphine so she could die. I watched her breathe, waiting for her to exhale. She never did. I was relieved."

Frequently Asked Questions

There are many questions that children ask. Examples of some of these questions are presented according to age categories.

Three Years to Five Years
Question: "Where did my Mommy go?"

The answer given should be one that a child is capable of understanding and one with which the parent is comfortable. The answer should provide comfort to the child. It is also important to remember that three-to-five-year-olds do not understand the concept of death.

The child who asked this question was not from a religious family and the father did not want to give a religious answer.

Answer: "I think Mommy is with the stars in the sky."

This child was comforted by the response. The child would often point to the stars and say, "That's where my Mommy is."

Religious Answer: "Mommy is with God in heaven" or "Mommy is with Jesus."

Less Religious Answer: "Mother is with Granny and Aunt Helen."

These explanations help a child to locate the parent. According to Silverman et al. (1992), "Making an effort to locate the deceased is an important dimension in connecting to the dead parent."[5]

Question: "Is Daddy sleeping?"

It is important to explain that death is not sleep and that the father will not return. If children associate death with sleeping, they may fear going to sleep.

Answer: "No. He is not sleeping. Daddy did not go to sleep. Daddy died. When we die we do not wake-up."

Question: "Will Mommy visit me tonight?"

Children often feel haunted by the dead and are frightened by ghosts.

Answer: "Mommy has been very sick, and she's not here anymore. She will not visit you tonight, but you can think about her and remember her."

Question: "Will Daddy come back?"

Preschool children see death as temporary and reversible.

Answer: "I'm very, very sorry. Daddy will not come back. I know it makes you sad, and it makes me sad too. I know you would like for him to be here with you again. It was not Daddy's choice to leave us."

Six Years to Nine Years

Question: "Will I die too? Will it happen to me?"

Answer: "Not for a very, very, long time, when you are very, very old."

Question: "Are you going to die soon too?"

Answer: "I will be here for a long, long time until I am very, very old." (At this point children need this reassurance).

Question: "Why did Mommy lose her hair?"

Answer: "The medicines for the treatment of cancer make people lose their hair."

Ten Years to Twelve Years

Statement: "I keep dreaming a tornado is sweeping me away."

Answer: "I think you're afraid of things like tornadoes, but maybe you're really afraid of all the sudden changes that have happened since Dad died. There have been lots of changes that you did not expect, just like the suddenness of a tornado. But, slowly we'll get used to the changes."

Twelve Years to Eighteen Years

Question: "Why couldn't the doctors make her better?"

Answer: "Sometimes, medicine is not enough. The doctors did everything they could."

Question: "Will I die of the same disease?" (Her mother died of breast cancer.)

Answer: "Genetic research is making enormous progress. I hope that a cure will be discovered soon."

CHAPTER 2

THE FIRST FEW WEEKS AND MONTHS

Changes and Adjustments in the Household

Although the traditional roles of husbands and wives are no longer as distinct as they once were, with a man as wage earner and a woman as homemaker, the following section will use these conventional roles.

The Father Now Alone

Traditionally, a mother is responsible for running the household: she delegates tasks, does chores, and oversees the smooth functioning of the home. The structure she provides is important to all children. Like a maypole from which ribbons happily swirl, a mother's role is to center and ground the family. With a mother's death, that feeling of security is lost. A quietness pervades the household, a silence Emily Dickinson described as " . . . the certain stillness that overtakes the house when somebody dies." The father is alone: He now has to organize it all.

Immediately after the funeral, the father is bombarded with details. He is trying not only to cope with his own grief and pain but to understand his children's emotions and a cacophony of household demands. The household that appeared to run seamlessly while his wife was healthy has now become chaotic. Practical day-to-day chores and tasks have to be orchestrated. The Mother Goose rhyme is wise and worthwhile in its instructive charm:

Wash on Monday
Iron on Tuesday
Bake on Wednesday
Brew on Thursday
Churn on Friday
Mend on Saturday
Go to meeting on Sunday[1]

All this work must be done as well as carpooling, grocery shopping, housecleaning, clothes shopping, gift buying, and monitoring home and friends!

The father's responsibility has increased dramatically now that he must assume the roles of both father and mother. From early morning he now has to coordinate waking the family, supervising the brushing of teeth, the washing of faces, the combing of hair, and choosing appropriate clothing, all in a timely fashion. He has to monitor the progress of each child—no dawdling in front of the television set or sitting with one sock on, no playing with toys instead of dressing, no interminable showers for adolescents or marathon sessions in front of the mirror or going back to bed. Now the father has to get everyone out of the house with completed homework, prepared lunches, and other paraphernalia. All of this before he goes to work!

Karen, a mature looking 11-year-old, refused to participate in any chores after her mother died. She felt abandoned and angry. Her inner turmoil was reflected in her care of her room as well as in the way she treated the rest of the house. Dirty clothes, underwear, papers, and used candy wrappers were left lying on the floor, under furniture, and strewn throughout the house. Despite her father's pleas, bribes, and threats, she refused to pick up her things. She would promise to change her behavior but was unable to carry through on her promises. Immobilized by her grief, she was capable only of self-gratifying activities. After many, many months of therapy she was able to begin to look at her feelings and behavior, and she was able to understand her anger and hurt.

Emotional outbursts are often intensified by a child's depression and pain. "I'm not wearing these leggings. I hate them! Mommy didn't make me wear them. I don't care if it's snowing." Or, "I'm not getting up. I'm sick. Leave me alone!" A child immobilized by depression may stare vacuously at a closet filled with clothes, unable to choose what to wear. Frustration often overrules patience, because the father has to leave the house to go to work. A child's depression often manifests itself in anger rather than tears. Breakfast is frequently accompanied by tantrums, negativity, hostility, and irritability. "I don't eat breakfast." "I hate this cereal!" "Why did you buy this kind of juice . . . ?" "I don't have to wash my dish. . . ." "It's not my turn to the fill the dishwasher. . . ."

Caroline, an only child of 13, had been spoiled and indulged during her mother's long illness. She had never learned to help in the kitchen and had been catered to in terms of meals. After her mother's death, her father, an inexperienced cook, prepared the family meals. Caroline refused to eat what he prepared and demanded special food. She raged at her father and demeaned his culinary abilities. The anger she was directing at her father, himself in a state of mourning and grief, was an expression of the anger she felt towards her mother for abandoning her. This was also anger at the father *for not being* the mother. She would throw a tantrum and shout, "I hate you, I wish *you* had died." It was this explosive family situation and the wisdom of a family friend that brought father and daughter into therapy.

Many older children absent themselves from home as a result of a parent's death. This reaction is an attempt at protest and detachment, an adolescent way of dealing with depression over traumatic separation. Angry at having been left, these older children show their own anger by leaving.

If a father is fortunate enough to be able to afford a housekeeper, he faces another problem. Children may resent someone replacing their mother and introducing a new regime. A housekeeper may be greeted with resentment, opposition, tearfulness, and hostility. The father then may have to deal with the housekeeper's complaints and chagrin.

When finances do not allow for a housekeeper, the father has to surround himself with a support group for those times when he cannot be available. Neighbors, friends, family members, and the occasional babysitter constitute such a group. Sometimes a family member such as an aunt or grandparent moves in to help. This arrangement has its own set of problems: The children resent not only the replacement of the mother but may also dislike the different habits, rules, and household management of the caretaker, who is seen as an intruder. They transfer all their unhappiness to this surrogate, causing further volatility and unrest in the family.

When rage and unrest become so intense, the father must be careful not to be drawn into the conflict. He needs to be aware that this is an expression of grief and that outside, mediating intervention is necessary. Hospitals, clinics, religious institutions such as Catholic Charities, Jewish Family Services, Lutheran Family Services, family counselors, and private practitioners can offer help, insight, and understanding.

Circumstances sometimes suggest that children be sent to live with relatives or friends, or be sent away to boarding school. If possible, these situations should be avoided. Children who are still grieving over a major loss perceive this decision as a further abandonment.

The Mother Now Alone

Traditionally, the father is the main breadwinner and financial support for the family, and the family is often dependent on his income. Finances often are a concern when a father becomes gravely ill: A mother may not be able to earn the sort of income the father normally did. There may also be sudden and unexpected financial expenses such as hospitalizations, extraordinary medical bills, or additional expenditures for caretakers or housekeepers.

Although secrets should not be kept from children, the magnitude of financial stresses should not be shared. Children should not be burdened with information that they cannot affect or with problems they are unable to solve. Rather, a parent should express concerns or worries about finances to other adult family members, friends, or professionals.

If at all possible, it is important not to disrupt children from a familiar and comforting home during the crisis. When a parent is very ill and the prognosis is bleak, the healthy parent may believe that changes in the family finances necessitate moving to a smaller and less expensive home. Preferably this move should be delayed as long as possible. A child reeling from the severe illness or loss of a parent will find such a move traumatic, the loss of the family home symbolizing the lost parent and compounding the sense of grief and mourning.

Unfortunately, sometimes there is no way around selling a home or reducing expenses by withdrawing younger children from private school or older children from college. When this decision is necessary, a parent needs to introduce the topic slowly: not in an overwrought emotional manner but in straightforward, simple terms. She should first prepare the child by introducing the idea that money is more limited now, but such basics as food and shelter will remain constant. In a later conversation, the parent may tell the child about the need to move.

Euphemisms and platitudes should be avoided: "I always loved this other little house; I know you kids will love it. Our house is just too big." Or "We need a fresh start, and our house has too many memories." Children are very perceptive and will see through false explanations. The danger lies in the surviving parent and child entering into a pattern of hiding their feelings in an attempt to spare each other hurt and pain, hiding emotions to protect each other. This is a burden that prevents children from dealing with their loss and grief effectively.

> Beth was 14 years old when her father, Sam, died very suddenly from a heart attack at the age of 45. Until then, Beth had lived an upper-middle-class existence with her parents and older brother. She had attended a private school, lived in a large house in a leafy suburb, and enjoyed many privileges. Her parents had entertained well, and her father had been captain of the golf team at the country club. "It was devastating when my father died. We were in shock for weeks. The changes were horrible. We had to sell the house, 155 Maple Avenue, and move into a tiny apartment. My mother had to go to work as a receptionist in a law office. My brother had to come home from his first year at college and go to work as a clerk . . . *a clerk!* Everything changed. My mom's snobby friends dropped her when the parties stopped, and only three or four friends stood by her. Some people were kind—the nuns at my school arranged a scholarship for me, so at least I didn't have to leave my private school. But my world was upside down and there was no Sam for comfort. That was the worst. No Sam to make us all laugh. That first year or two we were so unhappy, I cried myself to sleep most nights. But my mom was strong and talked with us constantly, and so we got through. I don't think I've ever recovered from Sam's death." (For information on financial planning, see Appendix.)

Returning to School

Communication with a child's school is vital. The school and all of the child's teachers should be notified of the parent's death and the anticipated length of the child's absence. Prior to returning to school, a parent should contact each teacher to discuss the child's emotional state and to make arrangements for any work to be made up, taking into account the child's emotional vulnerability, preoccupation, and probable difficulty with concentration and attention.

> Shortly after Arthur's mother died, he became disruptive during music class. The teacher admonished him, "Arthur, if you do that one more time, I'm going to call your mother!" Arthur, who was still deeply grief-stricken, was understandably shocked and terribly hurt.

Upon returning to school, children who are already reeling from a parent's death may be anxious and fearful about the schoolwork they have missed and the potential questions that may be asked about their absence. It is ideal if the surviving parent can personally take them to school at the beginning. If this is not possible, the parent should explain the reason why and make arrangements for a loving adult to accompany them on their first day back.

The decision about exactly when children should return to school should be determined by their emotional state. It is helpful for parents to sit down and speak at length with their children in order to determine how they are feeling, although it is not always possible to discern their emotional functioning. Emotional defenses, such as denying pain and loss or repressing sad emotions, may be all that is observed. In an effort to maintain normalcy, children may want to return to school immediately. They may rationalize that they do not want to miss the field trip to the museum or the soccer match against a competing school. This is a part of the denial. They want to be like everyone else. The surviving parent needs to recognize their needs and support their wishes, while understanding that the blasé attitude is defensive in nature. On the other hand, it should be appreciated that some children need a little more time to be ready to return to school: the inevitable comments and questions are difficult for some children to face. Severe malingering—more than seven days out of school—should not be supported.

> Susan, age 16, had a difficult time returning to school after her mother's death. "The kids in school were uncomfortable with me. I felt like a freak. Nobody spoke to me for a couple of weeks . . . it was really awkward."

After the first day back at school, the parent needs to make a point of sitting down with each child in the family to talk about his or her experiences. The parent needs to find out exactly what happened during the day and how each child felt. The parent does not need to be a therapist, they need to just listen, be available, be supportive, and be understanding.

It is important to note that, particularly in the early days following a parent's death, children may not be available for learning. Preoccupation, daydreaming, lethargy, and "tuning-out" are all characteristics of grief. Children may not be open to listening, concentrating, paying attention or focusing in the classroom. Memory may be affected, too. For example, children may not remember homework assignments, projects that are due, or quizzes for which they must prepare. Sometimes they will experience difficulty with subjects they never had trouble with before. They may, for example, suddenly struggle with math, subtraction or division, because it is an all too potent reminder of the loss they have just suffered. Though frustrated, a parent needs to be careful not to criticize the children for these school behaviors. When necessary, a parent may need to address a teacher's impatience regarding a child's lack of availability or seeming indifference to school.

Bedtime

"The wild things roared their terrible roars and gnashed their terrible teeth and rolled their terrible eyes and showed their terrible claws."[2]

Bedtime is a vulnerable time for children. School, activities, and friends all help to keep thoughts of the dead parent at bay during the daylight hours. Children may be happy and centered during most of the day but begin to show periods of distress at bedtime. When they are tired, that which had been able to distract them loses its power. Thoughts creep out of the crevices as sleep awaits. The repeated failure of the parent to appear leads to anxiety and worry. A seemingly cheerful child can suddenly dissolve into tears and baffle the caretaker with an onslaught of emotion. "At school, I was lively and bouncy in a perfect mood, but at night I would grab a teddy bear and cry myself to sleep," recalled Betsy 15 years after her mother's death.

Children can become clingy, tearful, anxious, and fearful; they can become afraid of the dark, of household noises, of ghosts, or of visits from the dead parent. "Will Mom visit me tonight?" "What will happen to me if you die?" "What was that noise?" "Don't leave me, I'm scared!" "I'm feeling sick, will I die?" "What if I stop breathing, how will you know?" "Can I sleep with you tonight?" "I've got a stomach ache; isn't that how Mommy got sick?" Simple reassurance and a calm demeanor are often all that is required. Patience, patience, patience is the remedy.

A child may beg to sleep with a parent. And for the exhausted parent, anxious to get the child to bed, it is tempting and expedient to give in. When a child is very, very upset, the child can be allowed to sleep in the parent's bed and be transferred later to his or her own bed. On occasion, sleeping in a parent's bed will not be harmful; in the long run, however, it should be discouraged.

Tina never knew her father. He died before she was born. Tina and her mother lived with her grandparents where she always slept in the same bed as her mother. When Tina was seven, her mother became critically ill and was hospitalized. When her mother returned to the apartment, it was no longer possible for Tina to share the bed with her. A neighbor who was a close family friend invited Tina to spend the night at her home, and she too allowed Tina to sleep in her bed. One night became two, two nights became three, three became four. When Tina's mother died a few months later, Tina refused to return to her grandparent's apartment. Instead she insisted on staying at the neighbor's house, terrified that unless she was there to keep watch, the neighbor too would die.

Josh explained to the therapist that his three-year-old daughter, Shelly, was inconsolable following her mother's death, particularly in the evenings. Shelly was three years old when her mother died. The therapist suggested that an item of the mother's clothing might serve as a transitional object to offer comfort at bedtime. John gave Shelly one of her mother's favorite nightshirts with which to snuggle. Shelly immediately insisted on putting it on, despite its awkward length, and happily skipped around in the trailing nightshirt. For weeks, the little girl derived enormous comfort from her mother's nightshirt, and bedtime became less traumatic.

Some Common Reactions: Guilt, Fear, and Physical Responses

Guilt, fear, and somatization are common characteristics of grieving children. It is common for children to be occasionally angry at a parent and wish them dead. Then, after a parent's death, they are haunted by the memories of such thoughts and wishes. "Do you remember when Mommy said I couldn't have the big panda bear I wanted, and I said 'I hate you, I hope you die?' Do you think that's why she died?" Memories of undone chores, being surly or impolite, answering back, behaving rudely, disappointing a parent, as well as secret unexpressed negative or hostile thoughts, are all common themes which contribute to feelings of guilt.

"I wanted to buy my mother a grandfather clock for Christmas. I had been pretty mean and nasty when she was first ill.... I was told she wouldn't make it 'til Christmas. But the clock was what I wanted to buy her for Christmas. So I waited to buy it. I was never able to give it to her. I lived with a lot of guilt afterwards." (Martha, age 11)

With tears welling up in her eyes, Janet carefully took out a handkerchief and said, with a little embarrassed smile, "I brought a handkerchief with me. I came prepared. I knew I would cry." Twisting the handkerchief around, Janet, now 23 years old, addressed the group.[3] "I've thought about this so often. I loved her so much, and I still do 8 years later. I feel so terrible about how I acted. I was so mean, so angry, so sulky, and so unkind. I feel so guilty, so very guilty about the way I treated her and she never said anything about it . . . she never complained or was critical of me."

Janet was the youngest of five children. Only she and an older brother were still at home while her mother was dying of cancer. After school Janet had to hurry home to care for her mother, cook for the family, and do the laundry. On some weekends her older sisters came over to help clean the house when they could take time away from their own homes, husbands, and children. As an adolescent, Janet felt resentful that she could not socialize much with friends or go to parties and meet boys, because she was expected to care for her mother and the household.

After her mother died, Janet became profoundly depressed, so much so that she punished herself by moving from her cheerful bedroom into the cavernous, dark basement. At 21 she entered nursing school, planning to devote her career to caring for patients in need of intensive care. Although her choice of careers was an unconscious attempt to re-do her past, her guilt and depression were ultimately only resolved by the work she did in her therapy group.

Ceil, age 26, was also responsible for caring for her mother who later died of cancer, but, unlike Janet, Ceil never displayed her frustration or resentment. Extremely close to her mother since childhood, (her father had died when she was 6) Ceil was devoted and dutiful. However, after the death of her mother, she tormented herself with guilt. "I remember wanting to go to the school dance, planning it, and then something would happen like my mother's fever would rise and I couldn't go. I remember thinking, 'Just once couldn't you be okay 'til the day after the dance?' I never said anything about the resentful feelings, but I'm sure she knew. I feel so guilty about that. She was everything to me. I adored her." Ceil, like Janet, chose nursing as a career.[4]

Children frequently react to the death of a parent by converting difficult emotions into physical symptoms. Children who are very depressed are subject to colds, coughs, flu, and a variety of illnesses. Research has pointed to the correlation between stress and a compromised immune system, which results in susceptibility to illness. Headaches, stomach aches, and all kinds of aches and pains are typical expressions of stress-induced illnesses. These manifestations may be very real to a child, and a parent should try to be patient or non-dismissive with the formerly healthy child but should try to tolerate somatic complaints, remembering that a stomach ache may equal sadness and fear, a headache may equal conflict. Such behavior is not necessarily malingering; it can be an expression of grief. After the death of a parent, children feeling vulnerable and preoccupied are also susceptible to accidents.

Although 10-year-old Chris was known to be a sensitive and caring child, he seemed outwardly untroubled by his father's death. He continued his usual activities, perhaps playing a little more than usual with his computer and video games, but otherwise apparently coping and adjusting well. Always a quiet child, he did not want to talk about his feelings, and the family chose to respect his wishes. Three weeks after the death of his father, he fell while running down an embankment and fractured three fingers. Two weeks later, he fell from his bike and broke his arm and shoulder. His reaction to both accidents was intense, overwhelming, and belabored. It was as if his repressed tears, hurt, anguish, and grief were abruptly released with volcanic force. While he could not cry over his father, he could allow himself to cry over a physical hurt. This prompted Chris's mother to seek psychological consultation for the family.

In a very young child, regression may occur. Speech may become infantile, toilet habits may regress. Soiling and bed-wetting may take place. A child capable of walking may want to be carried, a child who had previously fed himself may now want to be fed, and a child who had given up the bottle may now refuse a cup and insist upon the bottle again. A child may return to overly dependent behavior such as wanting to be dressed, bathed, and helped in a variety of ways. These regressions are emotionally based, and a parent should not react harshly, but rather be patient and understanding of this reactive and regressive behavior.

Conversely, older children may adopt pseudo-mature behavior. They may become fiercely independent in an attempt to quell the fear of being motherless or fatherless. Older siblings may sometimes assume the role of caretaker as a defense against feeling the enormous loss. In this way they merge with the deceased parent, comforting themselves by identifying with the lost parent, by becoming the parent. The loss is then not felt as poignantly.

Illness in the surviving parent can be traumatic for the child. "I'm going to lock the door and never let you leave," said three-year-old Shelly when her father returned home after a hospitalization, six months after her mother had died. Shelly exhibited many needy and fearful reactions upon her father's return. She was clingy, tearful, demanding. She insisted upon being carried and demanded to sit on her father's lap constantly. Wisely the father spent much time with her, continually reassuring her and providing comfort. He spent hours reading stories to her, playing with her, and taking her on all of his errands. Despite her father's efforts, however, fear of abandonment may continue to be an issue for Shelly and in the future she may need some professional help with this issue.

Storytelling

Since the beginning of time people have used storytelling as a way of imparting information, passing down traditions from one generation to the next, generating cultural pride, and promoting healing in the psychically wounded. After a death, families and friends often attend wakes or shivahs, at which time storytelling is used as a means of comforting the bereaved. "I remember when Bob. . . ."

For children who have lost a parent, the telling of stories is a technique that is both therapeutic and comforting: being told stories either about the beloved dead parent and/or being told stories about the lost parent *and* themselves keeps them connected with the parent, offering a way of keeping the parent alive for them. It is important for the surviving parent to offer such a helpful method to bereft children or adolescents. For one shining moment the parent is again very much present in their minds and the feelings of loss and abandonment are muted.

Abi, age 7 years, never tired of hearing a story about her mother and herself when she was two years old. Her mother leaning over her crib, while tucking her in one night, said "You're very cute." The child responded, "Oo derry toot." Abi's mother had loved the incident and had repeated it over and over to anyone and everyone. After her mother's death, Abi delighted in hearing the story from her father, grandmother, aunts, and uncles, and would beg to be told the story one more time. It was a source of great comfort to her: perhaps it boosted her self-esteem and sense of security knowing that her mother found her smart and pretty, perhaps it was just being reminded of the memory of the time she had been close to her mother.

Shelly was born in China and was adopted by an American family when she was a few months old. Shelly's mother died when Shelly was a few weeks shy of her third birthday. At six she is hungry for details about her relationship with her mother: "Daddy, how long were you and mommy in China? . . . Tell me about the trip back? . . . Did my mommy love me? . . . Did my mommy carry me? . . . Did she take care of me?" Her need to hear stories about the interaction between her mother and herself borders on insatiable. Her delight and happiness at the stories are heartrending.

Jeb, a musically gifted young man, was 13 years old when his father died. Prior to his father's death he had always enjoyed the family-story that predicted his musical abilities. Just before his first birthday, Jeb and his father were in the car. As they stopped at a train crossing, Jeb pointed his chubby little finger at the train and sang out "woo-woo." His father was thrilled and thereafter claimed to be the first to recognize the child's musical talent. After his father's death, Jeb's mother would always say, "Remember woo-woo" before one of Jeb's major music events or competitions. She felt the story gave Jeb confidence and used it as a good luck charm. For some reason, prior to Jeb's audition at a major music academy when he was 17 years old, she forgot to say the magic words. Jeb, nervous and edgy, yelled "Mom you forgot . . ." and before he could finish she was able to say "woo-woo." Reassured and smiling, Jeb entered the academy and had a successful interview.

Most children delight in hearing stories about their parents and particularly stories about their parents as children. There is a pleasure in knowing that their parents were once like them, making for a connection and identification. For the child who has lost a parent there is a hunger to know as much as possible.

John's father died when he was five years old. He would beseech his mother and his father's siblings to "tell me stories about Daddy when he was little." His favorite story was about the time his father, age four, got lost in a shopping mall. When a security guard found the tearful child wandering around, he asked him his name. The little boy replied with his nickname "Pinky-ponky." The security guard, for whom English was a second language, broadcast, "Would Mrs. Ponky please come to the Information Desk?" At this point John would dissolve into giggles. The story was probably psychologically comforting for John. His father also had once been a frightened, lost little boy separated from his parent. Yet his father had survived and grown into the strong man the five-year-old loved and remembered.

Emma, age 10, loved to hear the story of her mother's childhood antics. "Grandma, tell me the story of mommy and the salami," she would say whenever she visited her grandmother. Emma's mother had died when Emma was 9 years old. Emma's grandmother would happily reminisce and re-tell the story, deriving comfort herself from the memory of her spirited daughter: "A long time ago there was a wonderful little girl called Amelia. She had bright, flashing eyes and a mischievous smile. No one could stop her! She had such energy! She couldn't wait for me to come and get her in the morning. She would climb out of her crib all by herself and scoot down the hallway as quick as a flash. We called her "Speedy." Some mornings I would go into the pantry and find little bites all over the salami I had hanging there! I don't know how she did it, but that was my darling little Speedy! Determined, mischievous, and quick." Emma, herself not a shrinking violet, loved the story because it allowed her to identify with her feisty mother.

"My father died when I was two-and-a-half years old. He was killed in action. I have no actual memories of him, although I feel as if I do because I know so many stories about him from my mom and aunts and uncles. I've also always had a photo of him in his uniform next to my bed."

Frequently Asked Questions

Children come to terms with their grief by asking the same questions over and over again. Stability is established by consistently answering a child's repeated questions with the same answer.

Three to Five Years

Question: "Will you take me to school? I'm scared to go back."

Answer: "I'll be able to drive you a few times. Later, we'll have to work out another arrangement. I know it feels strange and sad to be without Dad."

Question: "Will you be here when I get home from school?"

Answer: "I'll be home a little after you get home. You will go to Mrs. J.'s house (a neighbor) and play until I pick you up. I'll call you at 3:30 to see how your day was and speak with you, or you can call me. Mrs. J. has my work number. I'm going to write down my phone number for you to keep in your pocket."

Question: "Will I have scary dreams tonight?"

Answer: "I hope not. If you do, come and wake me and tell me about your dream and we'll talk about it."

Six to Nine Years

Question: "I don't like the way she makes macaroni and cheese, it's too runny—why do we have to have her?"

Answer: "We need someone to help us run the house. Someone needs to be here when I'm at work. I know you miss Mommy in lots of ways. She made wonderful macaroni and cheese. No one can make it quite the same."

Question: "Will Daddy forgive me for losing his pen?"

Answer: "He forgave you a long time ago, he knew you didn't mean to lose it. You must remember Daddy always loved you."

Ten to Twelve Years

Question: "Is there something wrong with me? I keep getting sick."

Answer: "Sometimes when people feel very sad and upset they get sick more often."

Question: "Why can't I watch television when I'm getting dressed for school? Mommy let me."

Answer: "Because we have more things to do in the morning before school than we used to do. I have to get to work and I have to leave the house in good order before we all leave. We have to hurry in the morning. I know you didn't have to do this before. This is another way that you miss Mommy."

Twelve to Eighteen Years

Question: "Why do I have to do everyone's laundry? It's bad enough that I have to do my own."

Answer: "Things have changed. We all need to help each other. I'm sure you miss Mom in many ways. She took good care of us."

CHAPTER 3

DIFFICULT DAYS

Birthdays

Mourning is an unpredictable process, an ebb and flow of emotion. Within the same day feelings can fluctuate. A day that seems uneventful suddenly turns into a time of tremendous sadness, triggered by something seemingly insignificant. "I remember turning down an aisle in the grocery store and seeing Pepperidge Farm Milanos, and tears welled up in me and I found myself crying in aisle 7B. Those were my mother's favorite cookies," reported Angela, age 14, to her therapist. Unexpected moments like these are difficult to anticipate and prepare for.

There are, however, ways to help a child prepare for especially difficult days. Anticipation and planning can help ease the pain. We know that days such as Mother's Day, Father's Day, birthdays, and Christmas can be sad ones since they elicit memories of past holidays with the deceased parent.

Our experience has taught us that the most poignant day for a child whose mother has died is the child's own birthday. Why is this particular day so painful? A birthday marks the day on which one is born and so links the child to the mother both consciously and unconsciously for the rest of his or her life. There is no closer bond. We may not be consciously aware of this symbolic connection when celebrating birthdays; however, when a mother is no longer alive, a child is dramatically aware of the broken bond. This awareness makes birthdays particularly difficult for children whose mothers have died. The person who was there from the very beginning is no longer there. The profoundness of the loss is keenly felt on this special day. "My birthday's the worst. I wouldn't be here if it wasn't for her. I don't want it celebrated; it's a reminder of not having her. The emptiness. . . ." said Ruth, who was three years old when her mother died.

Pragmatically, the celebration of the first birthday following a parent's death presents difficulties not only for the child, but for the surviving spouse as well. For the younger child, the remaining parent has to plan the birthday and all its festivities. The parent is responsible solely for the gift buying, invitations, treats, birthday cake, and the birthday specialties. This responsibility makes the parent very aware of his or her own traumatic loss. Clearly with the older child, the parent is not as closely involved in all the preparations.

Several weeks before the actual birthday, regardless of the age of the child, the parent needs to have a conversation with the child about the upcoming birthday. In this way, the parent helps prepare the child for a birthday that is both different and difficult. There should be an acknowledgment that the child will probably have mixed feelings about the upcoming day. The child might be both excited about the birthday, but also sad that the deceased parent is not there. Together the parent and child need to decide if the child wants a party, what kind of a party, who should be invited, and what should be served.

> Arthur, age 10, vehemently refused his father's suggestion to bring cupcakes to school on his birthday. "I just don't want cupcakes this year. They're stupid," he said "And don't you come to school either." Later it became apparent that his reluctance had little to do with the cupcakes but rather that the entire class would now know he did not have a mother. His mother had died recently, and he was not yet prepared to deal publicly with his loss. His wishes were respected.
>
> Sheila's father died when she was three years old, yet on her birthday, six months later, it almost seemed as if she were oblivious to her recent tragic loss. Caught up in the excitement of the party, she never mentioned her father.

Even a young child needs to be a part of this birthday-planning process. In spite of the fact that one parent is no longer there, the birthday must be anticipated, acknowledged, and planned for. It must be as normal as possible. The manner in which birthdays were celebrated in the past should be continued: Some families have a simple family celebration, others have more elaborate parties, and some acknowledge the day without outward manifestations. It is helpful to try to maintain consistency with the past. However, if a child has strong feelings about not maintaining the sameness, those feelings, after thorough investigation, should be taken into consideration.

> From the time of Jon's first birthday, he and his father had had a special birthday tradition. His parents would wake Jon and bedeck his bed with presents. Then Jon and his father would go to The Pancake House for a special birthday breakfast. They always ordered blueberry pancakes smothered in syrup, something Jon's father had instituted because his father had done the same with him. On the morning of Jon's fifth birthday, four months after his father had died, Jon awoke vomiting. His mother, normally a sensitive, thoughtful woman, had not anticipated that Jon would react so strongly to the loss of his father on his birthday. Her own grief had been so overwhelming she had forgotten the birthday ritual. At first she thought that Jon was physically ill. Only after speaking with her own mother did she recognize the depth of his psychological despair. Had she anticipated his potential upset before the birthday, she could have talked with Jon and prepared him for sad feelings, for the missing of his father, and the break in the ritual. Together, perhaps, they could have decided on a substitute plan for the day.

Although one wants to protect children from pain, it is important that a missing parent's birthday also be noted. This acknowledgment is important because on the birthday the surviving parent may display some distress. The surviving parent may not even be aware of a mood change, but children are perceptive and easily pick up shifts in their parents' moods. To avoid misunderstandings, the parent needs to identify the reasons for the change in mood. Something as simple as, "I'm thinking about your mom or dad today. Today would have been her or his birthday" is all that is needed. A discussion does not need to be belabored. Should a child wish to reminisce about the past, however, a parent should be available. Sometimes a child may reject any conversation about the birthday in an attempt to defend himself or herself against pain.

With an older child or adolescent, the birthday of the deceased parent is usually sad. "It's my mother's birthday on Monday. I'm dreading it. I'll go to the cemetery, and I know I'll just cry and cry. I'm taking off from work. I don't want to see anyone." Patricia's mother had died 5 years before when Patricia was 14. Her mother's birthday remained a particularly difficult day for her. Visits with family members, engaging in comforting activities such as a walk with a close friend or visiting a house of worship may be soothing ways to deal with this difficult day.

Mother's Day and Father's Day

Advance planning for the day itself is helpful when traditions from the past are sadly no longer applicable. A few weeks before Mother's Day or Father's Day, the surviving parent needs to talk to the children about the approaching day, asking for their suggestions and being responsive to their emotions. Together they should come up with a plan that will be comfortable for the family. A visit to a zoo or museum, a picnic in the park, an extended family gathering, or an out-of-town excursion are all options. Conversely, there are certain places the family may want to avoid: restaurants specializing in Mother's Day or Father's Day brunches, church services honoring parents, a country-club event that focuses on the day, or any other place that overtly celebrates Mother's Day or Father's Day.

Some children may appear to be coping well with the advent of Mother's Day or Father's Day. However, a delayed reaction may occur. Depressive tendencies such as preoccupation, difficulty waking up in the morning, trouble sleeping, loss of appetite, social isolation, irritable outbursts, thumb sucking, and bed-wetting are all symptoms of distress. The behavior should not be ignored and should be understood in the context of the day and the feelings around the parent's death.

Mother's Day

"Every Mother's Day I close myself in my room with Dickens and a wet facecloth to cry once again over the death of David Copperfield's mother, emerging hours later, wonderfully refreshed. From the cradle every child fears his mother will leave him, and he is as bereft when she vanishes for a moment as if it were forever."[1]

"For me it's the very worst day. Worse than the birthdays and Christmas," said Caroline, age 19, as the Motherless Daughters Group discussed the approach of Mother's Day. Several group members immediately responded. Joan talked of her friends' unintentional insensitivity, as they happily discussed the perfect gifts they had found for their mothers. Ruth E., who had lost her mother when she was three years old, said, "And you can't get away from it—it's on TV and in shop windows, it's all over the place. It's like neon signs flashing 'You don't have a mother, Ruth E.!'" As each group member told of the hollowness of the day, the sadness leading up to it, we learned just how painful the weeks preceding Mother's Day can be. It is a constant reminder of what the person is missing and does not have.

Schools are inadvertently insensitive to motherless children around Mother's Day. From nursery school through grammar school, classrooms are abuzz with art projects for Mother's Day. Bulletin boards are plastered with poems to Mom, and an endless variety of paper decorations, napkin holders, cards, and devotional messages. For children who do not have mothers, but who want to be like everyone else, the sadness can be unbearable. Teachers and parents can be very helpful by being acutely aware of these children's situations and anticipating their vulnerability. They might, in advance, alert the children to the upcoming project and, together with the children, devise alternative plans, such as making cards for their grandmothers, favorite aunts, babysitters, neighbors, housekeepers, or sisters. The children then do not feel excluded or embarrassed by their unique situation.

After-school programs present similar difficulties for motherless children. Weeks in advance of the special day, projects are begun with zeal. Macaroni necklaces, clay ashtrays, papier-mâché bowls, Kleenex flowers, endless drawings, and self-portraits occupy hours and weeks of rainy April days. At every turn motherless children are reminded of their loss. Since preparations for this day are done over an extended time period, the bereft children may experience both mounting anxiety and depression. A father needs to be alert and watchful for changes in behavior because these often signal a child's distress. Like a detective, the parent needs to put the pieces together and respond to the child with empathy and understanding.

Father's Day

In order to protect her feelings, Rosie, an adolescent, denied that an upcoming Father's Day had any meaning for her. "I'll spend it with all my friends, none of them do anything for Father's Day. It's a stupid day! We'll all just go out for lunch." However, Father's Day turned out not to be a meaningless day for her, particularly when her friends changed their minds and were unable to go out with her because they were celebrating with their own fathers. Rosie spent the day in bed, depressed, and with a bad cold. She slept the day away. In spite of her avowed denial, the day was a difficult reminder that she did not have a father, a reminder of her pain, a reminder that she was different.

Andrea, an 18-year-old, lamented to her therapist, "It seemed so weird not to be buying a card, not to be racking my brain for something my dad would like, going through the anguish of 'I can't buy him another tie.'" She spent the next few sessions, tearful and distressed, discussing the sadness at not having a father. "He'll never know how much I miss him, what I've achieved, and how I look all grown-up. My children will never know him. It seems so unfair."

Holidays

Holidays are very trying times following the death of a parent. Hollywood and books have conjured up ideal holiday images of the mother bustling in the kitchen while the father and children joyfully interact with each other: A blissful family, contented and secure. After the death of a parent, this portrait of perfection is shattered. The holidays become bittersweet, reminding the family of the loss.

Regardless of the ages of the children, it is important for a parent to remember that, well in advance of each special day, the parents should talk to the children about the upcoming holiday and explore with them ways they may wish to spend the day. Time should be allowed for reminiscences. Time should also be allowed for the expression of feelings and for imagining what it will be like to celebrate the holiday without the parent. Denial and silence can complicate matters, sometimes igniting explosions when suppressed emotions can no longer be contained.

Traditional foods play an important role on certain holidays such as Easter, Passover, Thanksgiving, and Christmas. The mother's role is central to these holidays, for it is typically she who organizes the traditional meals. Her absence is profoundly felt on these special days, particularly because food symbolizes nurturance. Now it is not only the meal that is different, but all the accompanying preparations become fraught with yearning and memory: baking soda bread and shamrock cookies, dyeing Easter eggs and filling Easter baskets, baking pumpkin pies, making Christmas cookies, stringing popcorn and cranberries.

However, traditions can be continued, even though the mother is no longer present. The father, sometimes with the help of an aunt or grandmother, can accomplish many of the traditions or make alternative plans for the actual holiday meals, perhaps by celebrating in the home of friends or extended family.

In addition to food, Christmas is a holiday rife with accessories and embellishments. Christmas cards, Christmas trees, Christmas decorations, Christmas shopping, Christmas presents, Christmas pageants and Christmas ballets are all part of the season's celebration. In each of these situations, the parent is missed and remembered. The Christmas catalog with idyllic scenes of mother and child at the hearth bombard the family and are a constant reminder of the loss of the mother. Similarly, in families that have lost a mother or father, the annual Christmas photograph has been forever changed—it becomes a dramatic illustration of the loss. Even letters to Santa or Chanukah Harry are forever changed.

Dear Chanukah Harry,

Happy Birthday. I hope you have a great time with all your Chanukah friends. My name is Arthur Gold. I'm 10 and I live in Oaktown, Illinois and I go to school at Oaktown Elementary School. Say hi to Shlomo. I hope he leads the donkeys well through the night delivering presents to all the Jewish children. Also say hi to my mother Lynn Gold. My Mom died from cancer. I was only 10. For my wish I wish you to please do your best to cure cancer. I know you will try your best. Thanx, I love you.

Your true believer,

Arthur

P.S. I have enclosed a wish list.

Emotion is often seen at holiday-times. In young children, over-stimulated and overtired, and still dealing with their profound losses, emotions can escalate. There may be tears at the end of a Christmas day. This is often bewildering to the parent who has tried so very hard to make Christmas a good day, who has tried to compensate with perfect gifts. The tears often are for the missing parent, not tears of bitter disappointment over a gift. Parents should not be too impatient with what appears to be a spoiled child, but rather understand the genesis of the behavior. "I have this photo of all of us at Christmas that says it all! We're all lined up on the couch, all with lots and lots of presents around us, but no one is smiling. We all look so sad, it's an awful photo, really awful," sighs Ruth E.[2]

Denny was eight years old when her mother died. "Mom did beautiful wrapping; she was meticulous about wrapping presents. She would buy wonderful papers and ribbons and yarn. It would take her hours to wrap a present. Mom prepared for Christmas all year round. Last year I tried to decorate the house nice (sic). It wasn't the same."

"That first Christmas without him was awful," recalls Brendan, age 14. "My dad, my brothers, and I always went out to this little place to buy our tree. It was such a great feeling choosing the tree, struggling to get it onto the car, then driving home, often in the snow. My dad always put on a tape of Christmas carols. He always insisted on playing it real loud. Although we yelled at him to turn it down, that it was too soppy, we all loved it. It was such a time of closeness and togetherness. This year my mom and I went out and bought a tree. We both didn't say much, and even the guy selling the trees said we looked gloomy. On the way home we were both extra quiet. I know we were both thinking of him."

Easter brings sad remembrances as well. On September 11, Ian Thompson was killed. Several months later, his widow asked their youngest daughter what she was giving up for Lent. The daughter answered, "I gave up my father. Wasn't that enough?"

Many religions have an annual day of remembrance and mourning. Candles symbolizing the significance of the day are lit. In as simple a way as possible, a parent should explain the importance of the day. This conversation can be another opportunity to talk together about mutual mourning, allowing the parent to be open about his or her own feelings and giving the children encouragement to express their feelings.

Halloween is often a holiday where the deceased parent is really missed. Prior to death, the now deceased parent was pivotal at Halloween: Mothers helped plan costumes, suggested decorations, bought the candy and treats. Fathers often planned the excursion to buy the pumpkin and helped younger children carve it. Parents often accompanied children trick-or-treating. As with the other major holidays, the surviving parent must now plan Halloween alone. There should be no last-minute costume frenzies, blundered plans, or unavailability to go trick-or-treating. All of this needs to be carefully thought out and planned ahead of time. For the very young child, Halloween can be a frightening time because of the images of ghosts, ghouls, and skeletons. After the festivities, bedtime can be especially troubling. It is helpful for parents to spend extra time with their very young children both during the day as well as later in the evening after the trick-or-treating is over.

A few weeks after September 11, a five-year-old boy put Halloween stickers on his bedroom window "so my Daddy can see where I am."

The absence and loss of a parent are again highlighted on long holiday weekends, such as Memorial Day, Fourth of July, and Labor Day. These weekends are traditionally devoted to family and family activities. It is at times like these that the family feels their profound grief, loneliness, and difference. It seems like everyone has a complete family, a family with whom to enjoy the leisure of a long weekend. The Fourth of July fireworks, Memorial Day parades, and Labor Day picnics seem desolate without the deceased parent. As with any special holiday, anticipation, planning, and talking promote some comfort and security. Emotional reactions to such holiday weekends are to be expected.

Arthur, age 10, was very excited about attending the Fourth of July fireworks display. He urged his father and baby sister to hurry so they could be there in time for the very beginning. He didn't want to miss any of the display. Towards the end of the fireworks display, Arthur's father turned around and noticed that Arthur was nowhere to be found. After frantically searching for Arthur to no avail, the father hurried home hoping to find him. He found Arthur in the basement playroom, curled up in a fetal position, watching television. "You're not loyal," Arthur screamed at his father. Bewildered the father asked Arthur what he meant. "You were talking to the lady standing next to you, and you were having a good time without Mommy. I hate you!"

Special Events

"My mother was a ballet teacher," said Isabelle, age 14. "I remember her long, black hair that she brushed and brushed and swooshed up into a huge bun on the top of her head. From the age of 2 or 3, I was at the ballet studio constantly. I wanted to be just like her. I couldn't wait until I would be able to get pink satin toe shoes with the ribbons that criss-crossed across your ankles. I never got them. My mother died when I was 9. I stopped taking ballet at 10. The first recital after she died was horrible. I remember sitting in the dressing room and everyone's mother was there. They were fussing with their daughters' hair and costumes. I felt so alone. There was no one to help me with my makeup or costume. Suddenly, my best friend's mother said to another mother, 'Oh, someone needs to help Isabelle. You know her mother died.' I felt angry, embarrassed, and sad all at once. I decided then I would not go on with ballet. After the evening's performance, I never returned to the ballet school. Everyone questioned my decision. I just made excuses. Eventually, they stopped asking."

Isabelle's example is typical of a child who has lost her mother. There is something very special about the pre-performance excitement of a special event. Dressing rooms are filled with the sounds of mothers, giggling children, hysterical shrieks, soothing utterances, and last-minute advice-giving. For the children who have lost their mothers, this is an extremely difficult experience. This is a world for mothers and children only—the well-meaning father is not part of the harem-like dressing-room scene. A favorite aunt or grandmother can help, but it's not the same. It is an inconsolable ache.

When James, age 15, came into the therapist's office carrying his trumpet, the therapist expressed both delight and surprise. "James, I didn't know you played the trumpet." It was clear that James, who was not particularly communicative, was trying to tell the therapist something in a nonverbal way. At first he shrugged off the inquiry, reluctant to talk. Toward the end of the session he opened up. "Last night was the spring concert, and I didn't tell anyone, not even my dad. I threw away all the announcements so no one would know. My grandmother found out about the concert 'cause she talked to my uncle and he was going 'cause my cousin is in the band. My grandma was mad that I had 'deceived her and lied.' I got into a lot of trouble, and she made me go to the concert. I was so embarrassed. Everyone's mom was there, and I was stuck with my grandma. Don't get me wrong, I love her and she's real nice to me, but she's old. My mom was real pretty, and I was so proud of her. She knew all the other mothers. My grandma made me introduce her to everyone, and I felt stupid."

There is no pride equal to a parent's pride. Children aspire to make their parents proud. The sadness and emptiness of receiving a prize or an award when a parent has recently died is particularly painful. Despite a surviving parent's presence and pride, the child feels the absence of the deceased parent keenly. There is little a parent can do to compensate except to be open and speak to the child about what is happening. For example, a mother might say, "Your dad would be so proud of you. I know you're going to miss him a lot at the award ceremony. Remember, he would have been so proud of you."

Eighteen-year-old Chris reported, "My dad would come to all of the football games, no matter what. My dad was a very busy consultant, but he always made sure that he came to our Friday night football games. He wasn't a great talker, but we would always hang out together by throwing the football around. The day we won the state championship I had to leave the field. It should have been the happiest day of my life. I couldn't stop crying."

Mother-and-daughter or father-and-son events are annual occasions that affect all age groups. The end of the year school picnic is but one example. Children are faced with glaring reminders when a voice over a loud speaker bellows, "Everyone get ready for the mother and son three-legged race." To soften the blow, a parent should anticipate this and discuss beforehand how the child wants to handle such a situation: who would the child feel most comfortable with, who would they like to have as their partner? This event could potentially be upsetting, but if events like this are anticipated ahead of time and talked about, some of the sting of the occasion can be lessened. Sometimes a child tries to avoid such events. The parent needs to walk the fine line between pressuring the child to attend, or out of sympathy, permitting the child to isolate and exclude themselves at home.

Religious rites of passage are traumatic for the family when a parent has recently died. Much has to be planned and organized. In addition to making preparations for the festivities, a parent has to make sure the child has learned the religious rituals and liturgies. It is a bittersweet occasion when a parent has died; it is hard for the remaining parent, hard for the child.

> "In those last few months he kept saying 'I just want to be there for Paul's bar mitzvah,' said Roberta to her grief group. He died a month before the ceremony. It was terrible for all of us."

Graduations are also very difficult when a parent has died. Perhaps they are especially painful because graduations symbolize the end point of something that has been achieved after much time and effort. Some of the milestones, on the way to the graduation, may have occurred while the parent was alive, and the graduation is then shadowed in memories, a reminder of the parent's participation in all that preceded it. For the remaining parent and child, this day can be a sorrowful one.

For the motherless or fatherless family, other events bring constant reminders of their loss and sadness. Attendance at family or friends' baptisms, confirmations, weddings, graduations, and funerals stimulate feelings for the missing loved one. These are occasions when an entire family will come together to attend important events, and, for the family without a parent, there is recognition that they are no longer complete. In preparation for these events, it is helpful to talk about what it may feel like, anticipate yearnings for the deceased parent and supply the children with stock responses to questions or comments they may get from others. For example, someone may innocently comment, "Your mother so loved weddings." For young people whose mothers have died, this sort of remark can take them by surprise, rendering them speechless. Children usually freeze at such times and don't know what to say. The surviving parent can help their children by providing, in advance, answers to such scenarios, such as "Yes, she did love weddings."

> Jim looked angry. His therapist commented on his expression. Ignoring the therapist, Jim, age nine, headed for the dollhouse where he proceeded to throw the doll baby out of the house. Eventually the therapist was able to get Jim to talk about what was really bothering him. Jim had attended a family baptism over the weekend. "I was so jealous of the baby. It's not fair. It makes me mad. I guess it also makes me a little sad. That baby doesn't know how lucky it is."

Abruptly, Katherine, age 14, said, "I want to start first this week." With a sigh she continued, "Last Monday I went to my father's cousin's funeral. I didn't really know her very well, but she was a nice lady. My mom didn't want to go alone, so I said I'd ride with her. It was a gorgeous day, just like the day we buried my father. My mom and I were kind of laughing in the car, on our way to his cousin's funeral, wondering if his other crazy cousin would be there. We were fine. When we walked in and I saw my dad's cousin's daughter standing there, I started to cry. I couldn't stop crying. I didn't know my father's cousin very well, but for the entire service I just sobbed and sobbed. I don't know if I ever told you guys, I never shed a tear at my own father's funeral. It must have been that I was in shock, because he died so suddenly. It was like those raw feelings burst out of me, four months after my father's death."

"I have to give a wedding shower for my roommate, and I don't know where to start." Alexandra's mother had died when she was 15 years old. She had never attended a wedding shower and knew nothing of the customary prenuptial events. Naive and socially isolated since her mother's death, Alexandra had no one to turn to for advice, no one to tell her what a shower entailed, to offer menu or venue suggestions. Motherless daughters face such dilemmas frequently.

Planning for a wedding is always stressful. Planning for a wedding when a mother or father has recently died is emotionally wrenching. The bride- or groom-to-be is constantly reminded of the loss. The parent's absence is explicitly felt, particularly for a daughter trying to plan a wedding. Traditionally, the mother of the bride helps with guest lists, invitations, menus, flowers, music, reception places, and dresses. She not only offers suggestions, listens to ideas, and helps plan the events, but also offers support and soothes pre-wedding anxieties. The father's absence is equally painful. Who will walk the bride down the aisle? Who toasts the young couple? With whom does the bride dance the father-daughter dance?

"My grandmother arrived with a big box. Together we removed layers of tissue until we uncovered my mom's wedding dress. As I stood there, with her pinning the hem, we both just started to cry. We cried and cried. This was repeated again and again on my wedding day. When I came out of my bedroom and my dad first saw me, we both dissolved into tears. I can't say that my wedding day was really happy. There was such a void," sighed 19-year-old Jane.

Becky was 19 when her mother died. A few months later, she was cheerfully telling the therapist about her upcoming wedding. Asked about her attendants she replied, "My aunt, you know the one I always talk about? The one I really like. She's going to be my matron-of-honor." When the therapist started exploring Becky's choice, since the aunt was close to 50 years old, Becky began to cry. It became apparent that having her aunt as the matron-of-honor was Becky's attempt to have her mother in the wedding party.

Frequently Asked Questions

Three to Five Years

Question: "We don't have a mommy, how can we celebrate Mother's Day?"

Answer: "We can do something that Mom enjoyed doing with us, like going to the zoo. Or is there something you can think of that you'd like to do? We will always remember Mom on Mother's Day."

Five to Eight Years

Question: "Are we getting a Christmas tree this year?"

Answer: "Of course we're getting a tree this year. Daddy always loved Christmas and decorating the tree. We'll think about him when we decorate the tree and talk about him."

Nine to Eleven Years

Question: "Are we going to use the same decorations at Christmas?"

Answer: "Of course we will. Why do you ask? Are you afraid it will make you sad unwrapping the decorations and remembering? It's good to remember, even though it sometimes makes us sad."

Question: "Who will pin me at my flying up? The leader says your mom must come."

Answer: "Let's think together who's special to you. Would you like to bring one of your aunts, or Betty (a neighbor), or Kate (an older sister)? I know you'd like Mom to be there, but maybe it would be nice to have someone you really like pin you."

Fourteen to Eighteen Years

Question: "I don't want to go to the school picnic. Do I have to?"

Answer: "I think you may enjoy it, and there will be fun things to do. I know you'll miss Dad but I will be there. If you like, I can ask Uncle Joe to come, too. You always like being around him."

Question: "Are we going to have Thanksgiving at home this year?"

Answer: "This year we're going to Aunt Sally's house. I know it's different, perhaps next year we'll be able to have Thanksgiving at home again. This is the first Thanksgiving without Mom. We will all miss her very much and her delicious cooking. I know it's hard to do things differently, especially since there have been so many changes lately."

Question: "Graduation is boring. I'm not going! Do I have to participate?"

Answer: "Do you want to stay home because it's just me without your Dad? Why don't you think about it? Dad would be so proud of you, but it is your decision. I won't be offended if you decide not to go to your graduation. How will you feel in terms of your friends? Think about it; I'll support your decision."

CHAPTER 4

Do's and Don'ts

Talk, Talk, and More Talk

"He remarried very soon after my mom died. Kat was very insecure and young herself. We were never allowed to talk about my mother once she moved into the house. My dad and I would talk about my mother when we were alone out of the house. Sometimes I think he would make excuses to take me on an errand just so we could talk about my mom." Julia, a 50-year-old schoolteacher, told her therapist about the pain of the approaching anniversary of her mother's death. Although her mother had died when she was 14, almost 40 years ago, memories remained intense.

In many households, regardless of whether a parent has remarried or not, speaking about a deceased parent is often discouraged. The child picks up the message that any mention of the parent is potentially upsetting to the surviving parent and does not want to be responsible for inflicting additional unhappiness. Similarly, the parent attempts to protect the child from pain and so does not talk about the parent who has died, thus creating a joint conspiracy of silence. This unstated message was reported constantly in the Motherless Daughters group, as well as by individual therapy patients. This kind of silence is probably the greatest error that any surviving parent or guardian can make. Although it is often done for the very best of reasons, namely in an attempt to protect the child from pain, it is a mistake. The most valuable gift a mother or father can give to a child is to speak openly about the deceased parent, reminisce about the parent, encourage the child to talk about feelings, both good and bad, and to keep the dialogue open.

> "There was no conversation at the dinner table. We didn't talk about it, it was so taboo," recollected Ruth E. "The only time my father talked about Mom was once when I was a freshman in high school. Out of the blue he said something like 'your mom and I did the . . .' and I knew he meant *my* mother. I was floored. I felt good. I always tiptoed around mentioning her. I never wanted to hurt him. I think he never spoke about her because he was trying to protect us, too." Ruth E.'s mother had died when she was three years old. Until she was seven, she didn't even know her mother's name. Her father had kept a profile of silence. "I never remember him ever talking about her . . . nothing. He never mentioned her, not a story, not a reference, not even her name."

> Chris was eight when his father died. "No one ever talked about Dad's death. I grew up feeling we weren't supposed to talk about it. . . . I felt mad and sad."

Adolescents, in their typical defensive manner, often will not encourage conversation. Their parents should nevertheless pursue the topic with them directly. It is also helpful for adolescents to hear the surviving parent talk about the deceased with other people. This demonstrates that death is not a forbidden subject.

In an attempt to distance themselves from their pain, adolescents become silent. The silence is dangerous because the feelings are buried rather than articulated. Drugs and alcohol become a haven, a way to avoid experiencing the sadness. Adolescents also react by acting-out their pain through reckless driving, getting into fights, and challenging authority.

Retain Schedules and Structure: The Maintenance of Sameness

A parent's death is a wrenching upheaval to the family. To an already vulnerable child, any further disruption to the household or to daily activities is experienced as yet a further assault. Although it is difficult to keep things exactly the same, and changes are inevitable over time, the maintenance of sameness is ideal when possible.

The physical structure of the household initially should remain the same.

> "I remember coming home from the school, and the dining room was completely different. My mother had come from an old European fam-

ily and had inherited silver she was very proud of. It had been displayed on the sideboard. I knew the dining room looked different, but at first I couldn't make out what it was. Suddenly, it hit me. The silver was all gone. My mother's best friend (shortly to be my stepmother) had neatly packed it away in boxes, which were stacked on the stairs to the attic. She asked my brother to put the boxes in the attic for her. I was devastated." (Sonya, age 22)

Jenny was 10 when her mother died. "It was only three months after my mom died when he began dating. I was 10 years old. I remember one woman in particular. She was so bossy. I hated her. She would take pictures down. I would put them back up. She remodeled the house. I was miserable. I packed my things and moved in with my grandparents."

Emma was nine when her mother died. With an amused look on her face, she recalled how, as a young child, she loved to spend time playing with her mother's dressing-table accessories: the trinkets in the jewelry box, the silver-backed mirror, and the perfume bottles. Her expression changed dramatically when she went on to relate her distress at walking into her parents' bedroom shortly after her mother had died to discover a bare dresser. "I was bereft at the sight of the empty dresser. I felt as if I'd been punched in the stomach."

How long should a parent keep a spouse's most personal effects displayed? How long are personal mementos or clothing kept in the house? Frequently raised questions are: "What should I do with the clothing?" "When would be a good time to pack things away?" "Should I include the children in this project?" There are no hard and fast rules. The answer depends on the emotional readiness of the family. Certainly no changes should be made in the first few months, if possible, because children sometimes need more time to come to terms with this than adults do. Often it is important for a child to have something personal of the parent's to keep. Before packing up the personal effects the surviving parent should ask the children if they would like to keep something that belonged to their deceased parent.

Catherine, age 18, said: "I don't have many memories of my mom. She died when I was 9 years old. My one vivid picture is of her at the piano. She played beautifully, and I loved to sit next to her and watch her hands. My dad remarried very soon afterwards, and at first I really liked Meg. She was fun and took me for rides in her little sports car. Meg was much younger than my dad, and she treated me as a little sister or a young confidant. My dad was a big executive and often away. In fact, when she had her first child, she chose me to be her coach in the labor delivery room, and, of course, I was flattered. I think I was pseudo-mature, play-acting an adult role. No one was smart enough to realize

I just wanted to be loved. When I think of it now, I realize how awful that was for a kid—to be in a labor room. Later my dad lost his job so we had to move and sell off some things because money was tight. Without a thought, my mom's grand piano was one of the first things to go. I was devastated—it was one of the few things that belonged to my mom that we still had. It was then that I began to truly feel the impact of her loss. . . . I started rebelling with drugs and alcohol, and when I left for college, I never came back. In college I became interested in women's studies and later gender studies and started sleeping around with other women. I guess I was looking for a mother. . . ."

It was suggested to Arthur's father that a teddy bear, made from a piece of his wife's clothing, might be a comforting keepsake for the children. When Arthur's father told Arthur about it, Arthur rejected the idea, saying he was too old for a teddy bear. Many months later, two weeks before the anniversary of his mother's death, Arthur asked his father if he could have the teddy bear after all and tearfully selected one of his mother's shirts for the bear. Many years later, at age 14, Arthur still has the bear.

In an attempt to achieve consistency, daily routines need to remain constant. Initially, schedules should remain the same, providing a feeling of safety and consistency. According to Anna, "Meal times were the worst. No one spoke. Eventually I would simply take my plate upstairs and eat in front of the TV in my room. Even though the food was terrible, that didn't bother me. I couldn't stand the silence."

Showing Emotions

Overwhelmed by emotion and responsibility, parents in their own grief sometimes inadvertently strike out at the person they least want to hurt. "You are such a brat. You made it so hard for Mom at times." Spencer, age 17, reported his father's tirade soon after his mother's death.

"I was lying on my dad's bed talking to my girlfriend on the phone. He came in screaming, 'Get off my bed' and I said 'OK, in a minute.' He screamed, 'No, now!' And then he grabbed my ankle and tried to pull me off the bed. He really hurt me. So I started hitting and kicking back. All I wanted to do was lie on my mom's bed. It felt so good." Lisa was 12 when her mother died.

Children take their cues from their parents. Many times a surviving parent does not want to burden a child by showing sadness. Sometimes the parent is reluctant to expose feelings in front of the children, because the parent wants to present a strong image. Although one does not want to perpetuate sadness in children by repeatedly talking about a loss, one should not err and be falsely nonchalant or brave. Parents walk a fine line between the two. They do not want their children to pick up the message that emotions should not be displayed.

> Mrs. S. had expressed concern in family therapy that her son Ben, age 12, seemed almost cavalier in his reaction to his father's recent death. Ben replied, "How can you say I never show my emotions; *you* never cry." He went on to recall, "Even at the funeral you didn't cry. I saw!"

A grieving child often exhibits anger. Children and adolescents will both express irritability and anger when they are actually feeling sad. For a parent, this expression is often confusing. Patience, tolerance, understanding, and empathy are the remedies.

> Pauline, age 13, spent hours in therapy lamenting the absence of communication and affection in her home. "My mom never says I'm proud of you. My Dad was very affectionate and always encouraged me with praise. I miss him so terribly."

Realistic Expectations

> "People think it is going to be over in three months or a year," says Joan Gibala of the Widowed Persons Service at the American Association of Retired Persons. "They or their families think they should be better. But we often hear the second year is worse."[1]

Parents are often bombarded by schoolteachers, principals, camp counselors, other family members, friends, or neighbors exclaiming, "But it's been six months!" Arthur's experience with his camp director is typical. "It's very sad, I know, but really Arthur can't go on moping. It's been six months since his mother died." The camp director had requested a meeting with Arthur and his father following episodes of Arthur hiding during day camp. Mr. G. had been in therapy for several months and was able to explain to the camp director, in the child's presence, that there is no time limit to the mourning process and that Arthur was entitled to his sad feelings, which needed to be respected.

Initial mourning lasts a year. Thereafter the intensity lessens, but the prolonged pain and longing ache remain. Emotions are not logical and do not follow the structure of a man-made calendar.

"Boys scream, girls cry" is not always a realistic expectation. Some girls scream, some boys cry.

Sonya, a beautiful, ethereal young 22-year-old, bitterly told the Motherless Daughters group, "They sent me away to this boarding school. I hated it there. I guess they didn't understand those explosive tantrums were my way of weeping for my mother. I was only 8." Her family had unrealistic expectations about how a child was supposed to mourn.

A surviving parent should be sensitive to a child's personality and not expect a generic response. A phlegmatic, calm child may not display the emotions of a highly-strung, sensitive child. They may both have very strong feelings, but their expressions and adjustment may be different. The same is true of different age groups. A younger boy may feel it is permissible to cry, while an older boy may feel inhibited by social expectations. Again a parent needs to be mindful of such differences.

Premature Relationships

Reeling from loneliness and feeling overwhelmed by responsibility, many people find a companion prematurely. This is extremely difficult for a child or adolescent to understand or bear.

Mona's mother died when she was 16. Within a couple of weeks, her father, a wealthy businessman, moved in with his girlfriend, leaving Mona alone in the family apartment. The father sold all the furniture in the house, leaving Mona to sleep on a mattress on the floor. Mona felt her mother's entire existence had been erased. "I was numb but never thought to say anything to him. I finished the school year as if in a trance. It was only in my twenties that it all caught up with me, and I became very, very depressed and really angry at him."

"My father died in late spring," said 16-year-old David. "At the family July Fourth celebration my mother drove us all crazy; she couldn't stop talking about her new boyfriend. Each one of us cut her off, turned away, walked out of the room, and practically put our hands over our ears. She wouldn't shut up! We were all missing my dad so much. No one wanted to hear about her stupid boyfriend. It felt so disloyal, such a betrayal. . . ."

Grief Groups

Grief groups can be valuable in helping parents adjust to new roles and to lives without the support of their spouses. For grieving spouses, grief groups are both supportive and therapeutic. Ideally, parents are best helped by a grief group composed of contemporaries who have suffered similar losses and are dealing with the same painful adjustments. Raw emotions can best be expressed in a safe environment, where they can be met with empathy and understanding. Had Spencer's father had a support group in which to vent his anguish, Spencer may have been spared the painful encounter described previously. A group can also help parents to devise strategies for difficulties with children, housekeepers, and daily dilemmas.

> "The children and I are spending the Fourth of July with some members of my grief group and their families. We're going to the parade and then we are going to a picnic at the lake. I don't know what I would have done on the Fourth otherwise. My parents and brothers are going out of town and I just don't know what we would have done," said Richard to his therapist.

Grief groups can also be helpful for children. They provide an environment that demonstrates that people are not alone or unique in their grief. "My nightmares were horrible. I kept dreaming about legs." Twelve-year-old Tom's mother had lost her leg during her battle with diabetes. "The grief group really helped me. We talked a lot about nightmares as well as about our dead parents. That was the best thing my dad did after my mom died. He found us the group." Similarly, the grief group was very helpful to Janet, age nine, in preparing her for the first Mother's Day following her mother's death. Together the group members worked out a script to respond to the inevitable question, "What are you getting your mom for Mother's Day?" "Nothing. She's dead!" was the response they decided upon. This reply allowed the group members to express their anger at not having a mother using dark humor. It also allowed them to share their feelings and commiserate over their loss.

Some children, however, refuse to be a part of a grief group, particularly one connected to their school, because they do not want to bring attention to themselves or their loss. "I won't go to that stupid group at school. There's no way she can make me go," insisted Shannon, age 14. "It's full of creeps and losers, and I'd be mortified to be associated with them. Besides, it makes me different and I'm just not going."

Accepting Help

"Pride goeth before a fall." People often express the wish to avoid inundating family and friends with cries for help. "Oh, I can't ask her. She has three little children and she works. I know she'd help, but I've already asked her for so many favors." If people offer help, accept it!

Visits to the Grave

Many people derive great comfort from visiting the graves of loved ones. For them it represents a connection to the people who have died. If children or adolescents, however, are reluctant to visit a grave, the surviving parent should be understanding and not insist on their going. Only when the children are ready for this ritual should a visit be made. It is probably not wise to take children to visit the grave immediately following the death. Children, and probably most adults, need several weeks or months to accept, process, and integrate the loss. When the surviving parent feels that the family is no longer reeling from the death and has begun to adjust to it, such a visit may be suggested: "I thought that maybe on Sunday we could visit Mom's grave. Would you be comfortable with that? If you don't want to, I want you to tell me. We can always go later if you are not ready yet. That would be fine, too."

Cemetery visits should take place well before dusk or evening. Plenty of time should be allotted to talk to the child following such a visit. Acknowledging the sadness afterward is essential: "I know you must be feeling sad. You must miss Mom (or Dad) a lot. It's very sad for me, too." Even if children are quiet or chatter about something else, it is important to acknowledge the sadness of the visit. It is comforting for them to know that their feelings are understood, and it gives them permission to feel or express such emotions.

> Tricia was six years old when her mother died. "I know it sounds goofy, but I loved going with my dad to my mom's grave. We would take her favorite flowers and just stand there together holding hands. Sometimes tears would roll down his cheeks, and when I was young I would think, 'Wow! I didn't know grown-ups cry.' Later, when I could drive, I'd often go there on my own. I'd sit there for a chunk of time and tell her all sorts of things."

For the family whose loved ones have been cremated, there are no graves to visit. Yet having a place to visit can offer comfort. Sometimes these families choose to dedicate a tree or to plant flowers in memory of their loved ones. These memorials offer a place of remembrance, a place the family can go to in order to feel close to the deceased. Others plant a grove of trees, dedicate a bench in a rose garden, erect a plaque, or name a trophy in honor of their loved ones. Nothing grand needs to be done. Sometimes something as simple as planting a parent's favorite flowers in the back yard can be an effective remembrance.

Arthur Gold's mother was cremated. There was no grave to visit. The family decided to dedicate some trees in a local park in the mother's name. Arthur, who had shown little emotion at the time of his mother's death, became extremely enthusiastic and insisted on attending all the meetings with the park district. After much thought he chose apple trees, even specifying, the type of apple tree he wanted–Golden Delicious.

In writing this chapter, we have asked adults who had lost parents when they were children for suggestions and counsel for surviving parents. In the final analysis, it is the wisdom derived from experience that is the best lesson of all.

Suggestions for Parents: Do's and Don'ts

Christine James's father died when she was 8 years old. Now 31, Christine lists her do's and don'ts.

1. Strike a balance: A surviving parent must be both mother and father.

2. Learn how to listen carefully and read between the lines. "I didn't tell her anything that would be a big disappointment. For example, I was abused by an uncle and didn't tell my mother. I didn't have the language so I kept yelling "He's a Ni—" and got into trouble for using the word.

3. Express emotions. "I needed someone to be as raging as I was—someone to express feelings to and not to have to pretend that everything was manageable and OK. It's OK to have feelings: validate them. I cried in my pillow. She didn't, so how could I? I had to cry in private."

4. Allow for a healthy cycle of grief.

5. Let kids grieve as kids.

6. Parents need to grieve as adults.

7. Find a group that has suffered similarly so that there is a common experience to talk about what you're going through.

8. Remember religion and faith can be great comforts.

9. Don't ask children "How are you feeling" or "How are you doing?" I always said fine because I didn't know what to say. Rather, engage children in conversation.

10. Provide outlets. For example, try art therapy, grief therapy, or just drawing . . . because your feelings come out that way.

11. Be sensitive to a child with a new relationship. Don't bring anyone home prematurely. "Tread lightly; it's a raw zone."

12. Be discreet about sexual relationships.

13. It's important to be real and honest. "Let the child know you're dating, be conscious that kids are not stupid; don't say it's something it's not." Kids are intuitive and smart.

14. Provide a feeling of community. "Community—other people—is so important. [You] Need people around because it's a hole in your heart that you need to fill."

15. Tell the school. "I couldn't be quiet at quiet time . . . I was very disturbing to others chatting, walking around the room, preoccupied. The teacher said, 'What's going on?' I said, 'My dad died.' She said, 'That's enormous.' She got it! And then I could be myself again."

By the time Leslie was 18 both her parents had died. Leslie, now 35, lists her do's and don'ts.

1. Do reminisce about the parent(s) I've lost: It keeps their memory alive for me.

2. Do realize that people react differently to death.

3. Do share your emotions if you've lost someone close to you. It makes me feel less singled-out and alone.

4. Do be there to listen when a sad thought creeps up. It happens at the darndest times, and it isn't easy.

5. Don't be afraid to be yourself around me. I'm probably looking for familiar distractions to take my mind off things, even for a minute.

6. Don't alienate me. I remember my friends being nervous about asking me to go out and do things with them after my dad died, when all I wanted was to be a normal girl doing normal things again.

7. Don't keep feeling sorry for me. I'm probably doing a fine job of that on my own.

8. Don't give up on me. I'll come around in my own time.

Nick, a 49-year-old computer analyst, was tearful throughout his interview despite the fact that his father died 32 years ago. Nick was 17 when his father suddenly died from a stroke. For 32 years he has had sleep difficulties, abruptly awakening after only a few hours of sleep. The night of his father's death, Nick's mother woke him from a deep sleep at 3:30 A.M. to tell him that his father had suddenly died. This appears to be the genesis for the sleep difficulties. Following is Nick's list of do's and don'ts.

1. Help the children with their grief by being open and talking.

2. Don't support the denial.

3. Help the children with their guilt.

4. Help them integrate loss and grief into their lives.

5. Get the whole family together and let them cry—let it all hang out.

6. Let the children know it's OK to be angry. "I was really pissed at the old man for checking out."

7. Let them know it's OK to feel cheated.

8. Let them feel safe about talking.

9. Let them know it's OK how they grieve—everyone grieves in their own way.

10. If a child becomes spectral, pay attention and realize that something is wrong.

11. Give them time to digest and integrate the feelings.

12. Don't force adolescents to confront their grief.

13. Give adolescents a safe venue where they can express their grief—a gym, a library.

14. Be vigilant about unusual behaviors of the adolescent: sleep habits, agitated behaviors, drug habits, social isolation.

Frequently Asked Questions

Three to Five Years

Question: "Can I have Mommy's necklaces?"

Answer: "I'm going to keep them for now in a special place and when you're older you'll be able to have and wear them. But you can see them and put them on any time you want."

Six to Nine Years

Question: "Why do you keep talking about Dad? It makes me sad when you talk about him."

Answer: "I know it may make you sad, but it really helps not to keep feelings bottled up."

Question: "Can we bake a pie like Mommy and I used to?"

Answer: "I've never baked a pie before. I'm not sure I'll do it very well the first time. Let's get out Mommy's recipe book and we'll try together."

Question: "Can I have a photo of Dad for my bedroom?"

Answer: "Absolutely! Let's open the box where we keep all the pictures and choose whichever one you want. We'll get a frame to put it in."

Ten to Twelve Years

Question: "Why do I have to go to a grief group? It's stupid."

Answer: "I think it's important to talk about our feelings and get support for what we're going through. I would like you to come at least once to try it."

Twelve to Eighteen Years

Question: "I don't want to go to Mom's grave. Why do I have to?"

Answer: "You don't have to go to the grave if you don't want to. Maybe you'll want to go at another time."

CHAPTER 5

LATER ON

School: Fluctuations in Grades

Experts in the field of grief and loss know that grief is something we carry with us for a lifetime. *Children do not get over a parent's death.* They have to come to terms with the loss over and over and over again at different stages of their lives. The loss is never put behind them. It becomes part of who they are for the rest of their lives, not necessarily the part that is most obvious, but a part that is there nevertheless. No one has the power to undo the loss.

The inability to put a parent's death behind us is seen particularly in the school situation. Children show evidence of their grief for years: Focus and concentration are diminished, while intrusive thoughts of parents or associations surrounding them deter attention to the subject at hand. Anxiety over the loss of parents affects grades. Almost every school subject children study involves aspects that, at some time or another, will be reminders of the deceased parent. If the class is studying California, for example, a child may be reminded of a trip the entire family, including the deceased parent, took together. In math, subtraction or division becomes a difficult concept because it reminds the child of the loss. In English, much of the literature that is studied pertains to relationships, family situations, and themes of abandonment, separation, or loss. Even an essay assignment can trigger associations. A teacher attempting to be creative might ask the students to write essays on autumn, not knowing that this may be the favorite season of a child's deceased parent. The study of history is the study of the past, the past that included the deceased parent.

William Worden, in *Children and Grief,* studied 125 children, each of whom experienced the death of a parent. He found that a large number of children reported experiencing some type of disruption in their learning. Concentration problems were particularly pronounced.

> "My mind wanders. It wanders especially when we've been given an assignment and no one is talking; I just can't concentrate. I start thinking about my mom," Arthur reports.

> "Thinking really scares me. The only time I'm happy is when I'm asleep. At school I tune out. I can't care about my grades. My dad's always on me. I just don't care," Jimmy admits.

With this preoccupation regarding the deceased parent and the accompanying depression, homework suffers. Children cannot mobilize themselves. Often there is no one to remind them about homework, quizzes, assignments, or to oversee the work that needs to be done. A surviving parent returning home from work has a myriad of other responsibilities to take care of since everything now rests on one parent.

> "I spent hours on the phone from the moment I walked in the door after school," says Iris, age 12. "I fixed myself something to eat while I was on the phone. I'd chew in my girlfriend's ear and still be on the phone when my dad walked in. He'd immediately start screaming, 'Is your homework done?' Well, I was on the phone doing it with my girlfriends. But then he'd check and start screaming, 'Get off the phone!' I would scream back at him. He'd try to grab the phone and it was terrible. We'd fight, I'd cry, and sometimes it was so late by then that my homework never got done. I got Ds in practically everything. The next year wasn't much better."

Perhaps most baffling to a parent is the fluctuation in grades. It seems illogical that a child can get a B, then a D, then an A. This fluctuation is commonly seen in a child who has experienced the death of a parent: Consistency in grades is dependent on the ability to focus, concentrate, and attend to the material at hand. Sometimes even schoolteachers don't realize that these fluctuations in attention are part of the interminable grieving process. Teachers and parents want to believe that after a few months a child is no longer suffering, so they negate the length of the grieving period together with its associated scholastic difficulties.

> Mr. G. was called into a school conference. Several of his son's teachers were concerned about his child's low grades given his high intelligence.

"He's not working up to his potential. Last semester we didn't expect him to perform well, because we knew his mother had just died. But now it's been eight months!"

In an attempt to defend themselves against conscious painful thoughts, children may attempt to distract or comfort themselves. Cutting class, watching TV, talking on the phone, and sleeping are some of the methods children use. Many of these activities are desperate attempts to deny their pain by searching for pleasure and gratification. Iris relates, "I would cut class and go shopping. I would just buy and buy. Junky stuff. Sometimes it seemed to help. All I knew is that I didn't want to sit in class and think. . . . My dad got desperate and got me a tutor, and I would stand him up and go to the movies."

Guilt

It is common for people to feel guilt after the death of a loved one. Regret and remorse build over words not spoken, affections not shown, apologies never made, and the lack of time spent with the parent during the illness. Guilt can result in nightmares, attempts at self-punishment, accidents, or self-destructive behavior even decades later. When guilt appears to be causing a lot of distress, therapy is recommended.

Charlie, a 45-year old dentist, could not recall what his mother looked like. He was 18 years old when she died. Even with his therapist's urging, he was unable to resurrect any image of his mother. He had come to therapy because of multiple failed marriages. He recognized that something was wrong. During the therapy, it became apparent that guilt over his lack of attention to his mother during her illness was a heavy burden from which he could not free himself. He repeatedly married women in distress in an attempt to undo his original crime of not being available to his ill mother.

Jeanette, a 10-year-old, expressed guilt over not having apologized to her mother for her temper tantrums during her mother's illness. Several months after her mother died she began having nightmares. "My mother keeps calling me, and I'm watching TV. I go to every room in the house, and, after a while, I get frantic when I can't find her. I start screaming, 'I'm sorry! I'm sorry!' Then I wake up."

"I've always felt so guilty about my mother's death," 18-year-old Georgina confided. "My mom and dad got divorced when I was 5. When I was 7, my mom remarried. I liked my stepfather. He was fun and always brought me little treats. He always said, 'How's my little princess?' When they said I was going to have a little brother or sister, I was furious. I liked the attention of being an only child. I liked being the little princess. I didn't want to share them. At night I used to wish there wouldn't be a new baby. One day my grandmother picked me up from school after recess. At first I was excited. But my grandma acted kinda strange, so I knew something was wrong. Much later they told me that my mother had died giving birth. I didn't want anything to happen to my mom, I just didn't want there to be a baby. For years I've felt so guilty, like somehow my wishing it caused it."

"I remember all those flames. My mom was running engulfed in fire." Allan's mother, five months pregnant, had been cooking at the stove on a hot summer day when her apron caught fire. Frightened, she ran out of the house with the flames chasing her. Her two sons had been playing in the yard. Some 30 years later, Allan stood paralyzed as he watched a car engulfed in flames outside his garage. The memory of his mother, one that he had tried to keep hidden, raced before his eyes. The guilt at being unable to save her had plagued his every action for years—he was immobilized and ineffectual whenever anyone needed him.

Christine James did not know that it would be the last time she would see her father alive. "I kinda hugged him, and as I was leaving he said 'I love you, Pumpkin.' I just didn't say anything. It's my only regret in life really. I remember this memory of all the memories."

New Relationships

New relationships can be difficult for everyone. The parent who has been without a companion, without a sexual partner, without someone to share the problems of life with, who has felt solely responsible for a sick spouse, the children, a household, and income is exhausted. It is only natural that, after an initial grieving period, he or she will want a partner.

The need for a companion, however, can also be accompanied by tremendous feelings of guilt, ambivalence, disloyalty, and concerns about the family's reaction. Although young children are often initially excited and happy, as we will see in the example of Katherine, older children frequently have a difficult time adjusting to the parent's new relationship. Their sadness and anger over the death of their parent is often displaced and targeted onto the intruder.

Katherine's mother died when she was five years old. She was an only child. "My father married my first-grade teacher. It was a big deal to be normal like everyone else, so I was excited to have her in the house. And then the trouble started. She was abusive, physically and emotionally; she was jealous and threatened by me. She was pretty nasty to me. I even had to do my own laundry when I was real little. For a long time I was convinced there was something wrong with me. She was afraid of my dad and I [sic] being together, afraid of what we would say to each other. I was never allowed to mention my mom, and everything of my mother's was taken out of the house. In high school I decided if life was going to get better I needed to leave.

After she and my dad had children together, she became even meaner, like the original wicked stepmother. She would intentionally serve dinner before I got there. She would buy me the cheapest clothes and dress her own kids well. I had to work to put myself through college, but there was money for hers [her children]."

After a certain period of mourning, it is normal for a surviving parent to seek new friendships. This should be done in a delicate and subtle manner, without initially involving the children. The children are already struggling with their loss and do not need the added pressure and disruption of further change. A parent needs to be circumspect at this time because children see and hear everything.

Very shortly after Arthur's mother died, he was on an outing with his father when they met a neighbor in the parking lot. Arthur later confronted his father, "I hate you! I saw you kissing her in the parking lot. You're disloyal and you don't love Mom anymore! Don't you dare see that horrible woman again. I hate her!"

"My mother's first relationship after my father died was with a doctor with grey hair. I couldn't imagine how my young, cute mom could be with him. He used to say, 'How are you doing?' I thought, 'Relax, I'm just a kid.' Mom was enamored with him. I used to sleep in Mom's bed until she came home after a date. That lasted until I was 13. I was always concerned that she wouldn't come home. The lights were always switched off after Mom got home. Once, when I awoke in the middle of the night, the lights were on, so I walked into my room thinking she wasn't home yet. I had a canopied twin bed. I clearly knew someone was in the bed. This man said, 'You have to leave.' I screamed, 'You're hurting her. Oh, my God, what are you doing? Get him out of here.' I never saw him again. She didn't date for a while," laughed Ginny.

No matter how long an illness lasted, a surviving parent should be sensitive about rushing a stranger into the household. Children need a prolonged period of adjusting, not only to their parent's death, but also to the introduction of a new person into the household. "I remember this very pretty lady giving my twin and me a lollipop at the funeral. We didn't know who she was. My dad married her six weeks later. The next day my brother ran away," reported Maureen, age 15.

Only when the parent becomes seriously attached to someone and is contemplating marriage should they introduce their future spouse to their children. This introduction should be done gradually. For example, "I met a very nice friend that I'd like you to meet. I think you'll like this person. My friend has heard so much about you and wants to meet you. It might be fun for us to go to dinner together."

Children attend a first meeting such as this one with a variety of feelings. They may be fearful of losing their parent, anxious that the new person won't like them, guilty that they are betraying the deceased parent if they like the person, and angry at the parent's new attachment. "I know I annoyed him. I felt his sense of annoyance. I know he didn't like me," said Ann, age 17.

Some children may be polite at the meeting, some may be quiet, some may be rude, some obnoxious and surly, while others may attempt to embarrass the parent or the significant other. Parents should neither overreact nor be governed by their children's initial reactions. They should talk to their children, give them assurance, and spend a great deal of time with them, helping them to adjust to the new situation. If the process is rushed, the consequences could be disastrous.

> After his father's hasty remarriage, Ted, age six, felt abandoned by his father and felt resentment toward his stepmother. Neither adult recognized the child's despair. His father showed little understanding of Ted's anger, hurt, or sadness. The child felt he could not show his true feelings. His emotions were then expressed through encopresis (soiling). The honeymoon couple returned home to find feces spread across the front hallway and bedroom.

Someone entering this tricky situation needs to be aware of the children's vulnerability and their mixed emotions. Children's comments and actions should not be taken personally but rather should be understood in a broader context. Patience, tolerance, and sensitivity are essential. A sense of humor and irony are helpful. *Kindness is paramount!*

A wicked stepmother or stepfather can torment children for life, affecting their emotional well-being and coloring their perspective forever. When a parent sees or hears discord between the children and the step-parent, family therapy should be immediately pursued. In this way, much pain and unhappiness can be prevented.

Ruth E.'s mother died when she was three, and her father remarried a short time later. "As much as I hated her, I struggled to win her love. I was afraid of her. . . . She made sure there was no food in the house when we came home; she didn't want us there. I got the flu every December, I even missed being the Virgin Mary [in the Christmas pageant], not that she'd ever take care of me . . . I wasn't allowed to go out to play. I had to stay in and iron her pajamas and pillowcases when I was still a little child . . . I had to sign my Social Security check over to her . . . I remember when she said, 'You girls have to pay rent.' I worked in a florist so that I could earn money to pay for high school, because she wouldn't let my dad give me the money. She wouldn't go to my sister's wedding because they hadn't put her name in the paper. I remember trying to please her, never disrespecting her. It was terrible on Mother's Day . . . it hurt to go to friends' houses and see them with their mothers. . . . When I first went to college I had to take the bus— she wouldn't even let my dad drive me."

"At first I liked her. She was trying to get me to like her, but I didn't feel she was sincere. Then she became really mean. I remember going to wash my hair one morning, and I didn't realize I'd run out of shampoo. I went to the hall closet, 'cause that's where the shampoo was kept. Not thinking anything of it, I left the bottle in my shower. When I came home from school she yelled at me. 'Why did you use *my* shampoo? You took it without asking. You are never to use anything of mine again.' I never did," said Emma, age 16.

Ken bitterly recounted, "She was always favoring her children over me. I hated her. My older sister ran away at 17. They used to get into knock-down, drag-out fights over how she favored her own kids over us. My dad never stood up for us. I was only 4 when my mother died. I never felt I had a mother."

"My dad married my mom's best friend. At first she acted as if she really cared about us, but that changed in short order. She was a bitch! Looking back, I realize she was always jealous of my mom. My mom was the archetypal Scandinavian beauty. She hated me because I looked like my mom. There were three of us kids and we were close. She was always trying to divide us and make us angry at one another. Sometimes it worked. She would pit one against the other. She even tried to alienate us from our dad. She would make up stories about his misdeeds. It was terrible. As soon as she moved in, she took down all the photos of my mom. She took all my mom's jewelry. Even when I became an adult, my father and I had to scheme in order to see one another. I never call him at home, because she listens in on our conversations. I only call him at his office. He can never tell her that he's meeting me. Even 15 years after my mom's death, she is still jealous," recalled Sonya, age 23.

Theo, a lawyer of 40, had an abusive, resentful stepfather who demeaned him, teased him, and physically abused him. Theo's father died when he was 5 years old. A couple of years later, his mother married a policeman. "So began the torture. He called me a mommy's boy, bullied me about anything and everything, and when I was 17 and six feet tall, beat me up so badly that I landed in the hospital." Theo suffers from post-traumatic stress syndrome and has had work-related difficulties with male authority figures.

Of course, there are children who have positive feelings about their stepparents. "My mother died when I was eight. My dad married my mom's sister. She was wonderful to me. She treated me like I was her own child. She told me stories about my mom growing up and what she was like as an adult. I don't remember her so well, but my aunt filled in the memories for me. I can't imagine life without my aunt. She was a fairy godmother, not a stepmother," said Jillian, age 18.[1]

"My mother married George when I was four. George has always treated me like a son. I still have the stuffed lion he gave me at our first meeting! Apparently, when my mom told me that she was going to marry George, I was so excited that I went round to all the teachers at my nursery school and told them 'We're getting married, George and Mommy and me!'

Even though George and my Mom had three more children I never felt like I was different in the family. In fact when George got two tickets to the Superbowl he took me and not my younger stepbrother because I was the oldest son! I love that man." (Nicholas, age 19)

Emotional Reactions

Studies have found that social withdrawal, social isolation, depression, and a lowered sense of self-efficacy are evident after a parent has died. The full impact of the loss may not be felt immediately. These symptoms have been seen as late as several years following a parent's death. Over time, the absence of the parent in situation after situation is felt all the more keenly. The cumulative effect of not having a mother to help with your homework, cooking the family dinner, or soothing you when you become ill crystallizes the magnitude of the loss. The cumulative effect of not having a father to add strength and protection, attend sports events, and be a strong presence in the household compounds as time goes on. It begins to sink in that the parent is never returning. This realization makes the depression increase over time.

With tears in her eyes, Liz, age 19, said, "After my mother died, my grandmother raised me. I was 6 years old when my mother died. I didn't want to go to school. I almost failed a grade. I didn't want to leave my grandmother. I was afraid something would happen to her while I was at school. Time stood still for me when she got sick. I checked on her all the time. I think my depression got worse as time went on. By the time I was in high school, I was writing suicide notes. In college I stopped going to class, I cried all the time, I withdrew into myself. It was at this time the grief counselor sent me to a grief group. It saved me."

As noted in earlier chapters, acting-out and self-destructive behavior are often part of the grieving process. The behaviors should be taken seriously and be addressed immediately for they are manifestations of the grief and depression. Behaviors such as having accidents, drinking, using drugs, doing daredevil activities, driving recklessly, participating in risky ventures, cutting classes, ignoring school deadlines and rules, being involved in antisocial groups, lying, shoplifting, stealing, cheating, truancy, acquiring weapons, or any other drastic change in behavior should be taken very seriously. Similarly, changes in a child's standards of hygiene, dress, and presentation should be noted.

In a stormy father and son therapy session, Jonathan, a 15-year-old, blurted out, "You lied about Mom's sickness. You said it was the flu. You said she'd get better. You're nothing but a rotten liar." With this Jonathan started to weep. Jonathan and his father sought the help of a therapist after Jonathan was suspended from school for repeated truancy and lying.

"My mother was diagnosed with breast cancer when I was 5," said Josh, age 17. "When I was 14 she was diagnosed with leukemia, and she died when I was 16. I couldn't rely on anyone. I always felt like an outsider looking in. After she died my grades slipped. I got Ds. I had been a good student. I was very depressed in high school. I felt I had killed her. My father blamed me for my mother's death. He said, 'You're such an awful kid. She had no will to live because of you.' I really thought I'd killed her. I drove my car into a brick wall, but I only broke my hand."

Difficulty with attachments is common in children who have lost a parent. In our Motherless Daughters groups this was a persistent theme. Attachments and new relationships were constantly being tested and pushed to the limit. Having been abandoned by their mothers, there was a tremendous fear of being abandoned by yet another loved one. The ability to trust became diminished and the fear of further loss constant. The feeling of hurt surrounding the loss never goes away.

> Kerry was five when her mother died. At the time of her mother's death, she showed no immediate reaction. The family attributed her lack of emotion to her young age. A few years later, though, after a close friend's family was transferred out of state, her father became concerned about a shift in Kerry's behavior. She began to break off long-term friendships and refused all invitations to participate in group activities. In therapy, it became apparent that Kerry was protecting herself from the possible pain of losing yet another person she cared about. Having lost her mother and then a friend, she was terrified of any further loss.

> Christine James said commitment was one of the hardest things for her after her father's death. "As soon as boyfriends would start talking commitment, I was out of there! Therapy helped me understand that, but before therapy I would flee . . . I wasn't going to be abandoned again. I'd leave first."

While some children react to the loss of the parent by withdrawing into social isolation, others, particularly adolescents, take a different route and become hypersocial, bringing an almost frenetic quality to their social activity. They are constantly on the phone or out of the house day and night, insuring that they are never alone to deal with their loss and painful thoughts. Leslie illustrates this situation: from the time she arrived home from school she would be on the telephone to her girlfriends while eating, doing homework, or just filling the hours until bedtime. On weekends she stayed out of the house all day and night, making sure she slept over at a friend's house, never allowing for any quiet time. She was constantly on the go, whether shopping, going to movies, or rollerblading. Her behavior was frantic, with hardly a pause between activities.

Family Illnesses

It is particularly traumatic when the surviving parent becomes ill. The children's greatest fear has become a reality: They will lose their only parent. Children need enormous reassurance, support, and information to quell their fears. It is also upsetting, but not as traumatic, when a sibling, grandparent, or beloved aunt or uncle becomes ill. "After my dad died, I was terrified of my mom dying. I was fearful I was going to be alone. Every night I prayed that she would not die until I was an adult," noted Christine James.

Shortly before the first anniversary of the death of Arthur's mother, Arthur woke up one morning to find his father gone. He became hysterical. His grandmother had to tell him that his father had been hospitalized. Arthur needed much reassurance from his grandmother. When his father returned home from the hospital, Arthur's baby sister, age three, greeted the father by saying, "I'm going to lock the door and never let you out."

Frequently Asked Questions

Three to Five Years

Question: "Are you angry 'cause I hurt you with my trike? Are you going to the hospital? Will you die?"

Answer: "No. I'm not going to the hospital. No, I'm not going to die. Even if I were angry, I would never leave you."

Question: "You're sick. You were sneezing. I'm scared. Are you going to die?"

Answer: "People get better from a cold or the flu. People only die from very, very, very serious sicknesses. Since I've only got a cold, I'm not going to die."

Six to Nine Years

Question: "Are you going to marry her? I hate her!"

Answer: "I miss Mom lots. It will be some time before I want to marry again, but I do need friends because I need the kind of adult companionship that Mom and I had."

Ten to Twelve Years

Question: "What's the big deal? I flunked a test and missed two assignments. My teacher isn't worried. He said I can make up the assignments."

Answer: "This is a pattern that seems to have developed since Dad died. I think you're feeling badly about his death. It looks like you're having a difficult time concentrating. We can sit down after dinner each night and check your assignments and when they're due. If you need some help with your work, I'm here for you."

Question: "All my friends take little things from the drugstore. So what if I got caught? I gave it back!"

Answer: "I think you're missing Mom and trying to make up for what you don't have by taking things that might make you feel a little bit better. We can talk about how much you miss Mom, but I will not tolerate stealing or any other behavior like that."

Twelve to Eighteen Years

Question: "Everyone talks on the phone while they do their homework. My grades are still good, so what's the problem?"

Answer: "If you continue to talk on the phone for hours, your grades will suffer. You and Mom used to talk lots, and this might be your way of trying to fill the emptiness. It's fine to talk to your friends, but you carry it to an extreme.

Question: "Do I have to go to your wedding?"

Answer: "I would very much like you to be there. I know this is hard for you, but it's important to me that you be there because you are very important in my life. If you don't want to come, I will have to accept that."

CHAPTER 6

SUICIDE AND UNEXPECTED
DEATH

Explanations

How do you explain to children that their mother or father has killed themselves? How do you explain the inexplicable? How can you get angry or how can you grieve after someone has taken his or her life?[1] Perhaps, the gentlest approach is to focus on the physiological: to point out that brain chemicals are out of balance at the time of the suicide. Simplistic explanations are the easiest to process: the person " . . . has suffered from a special sickness of the mind . . ." or " . . . a special sickness of thinking and feeling." Different explanations of suicide are appropriate for different age levels. To very young children, under the age of five, only the simplest of explanations should be given; "Mommy died." After the age of five, a direct, but simple reason should be given because the child will inevitably hear the truth from someone else. As painful as it is for the child to know of a parent's suicide, it is more painful to be lied to and feel betrayed and unable to trust the surviving parent. A thoughtless or malicious remark can shatter a child forever. The details of a suicide should only be given to much older children who may ask many questions.

Secrets and Mysteries

Kevin, a 28-year-old professional, sought therapy because of a long history of insomnia. Once he was asleep, he would awaken some 30 times during the night. Kevin's father had died when he was a child.

Slowly Kevin and his therapist began the detective work of putting the pieces of the past together. It became apparent that Kevin feared falling asleep because of a dread that he would die. He recalled being told that "Father is asleep now," so he felt he needed to maintain watchfulness and vigilance. His insomnia was clearly related to the explanation he had been given of his father's death.

On further investigation, it became apparent that there was a secret surrounding the father's death. Kevin recalled that when he was 15 he had found a locked box in the basement containing his father's death certificate; the stated cause of death was different from the one given to him by his mother. His father had committed suicide. He never challenged his mother although he felt betrayed by her. Later, this lack of trust generalized to all women, and Kevin found it difficult to maintain close relationships with women despite his good looks and charm.

When a parent commits suicide, explanations are often vague, and a mystery surrounds the death. This is particularly the case when children are young. Parents often attempt to protect their children, fearing that suicide is too frightening a concept for them to grasp. Death is difficult enough to understand. Suicide is almost incomprehensible. Kevin, who was three when his father died, illustrates this perfectly. Family secrets, myths, and mysteries always result in problems, including anxiety, worrying, and issues with trust. The impression a child receives is that there is something so terrible and so dangerous that it cannot be spoken of; it looms like a black cloud overhead.

> Bob's wife claimed, "He wants nothing to do with psychology or therapy. He dismisses all of it. He had a terrible childhood. When he was 8, his mother was institutionalized for depression. She eventually committed suicide. He only found out when he was in his early twenties. He thinks Jane [their daughter] is like his mother and refuses to believe anything can be done to help her. He's given up on our daughter just like his mother gave up on herself. Our daughter [age 20] has never been told how her grandmother died. It's always been a family secret. Do you think it has relevance to Jane's problem?"

When a parent commits suicide, the overriding issue for the children is the feeling of abandonment, betrayal, and fear. Parents are supposed to love, not leave. Parents are supposed to be strong, not weak. Parents are supposed to solve problems, not give up. Parents are supposed to be there, not disappear. Parents are supposed to follow Biblical teachings such as the Ten Commandments, not break them. A child is left with a confusing set of messages when a parent commits suicide.

> Sadly, Olivia reported, "My mother told me my father had died in an accident. I was only five at the time. I never questioned it. When I was eight or nine, my friend, who lived next door, told me that my father had shot himself. I felt such an intense sense of betrayal. I felt I'd been deceived. Even though I later realized my mother was trying to protect us, I felt she had lied to us. I felt I could never trust her or anyone again. I felt so betrayed by my dad, too, so shamed. I was in Catholic school and suicide was a sin."

Reactions: Guilt, Anger, Shame

After a parent commits suicide, the family is devastated and searches for explanations. A myriad of conflicting reactions arise within a family unit. One child may blame the surviving spouse, another expresses intense anger, another withdraws. All are bereft at being left in such a violent way. Most children feel guilt that they somehow could have prevented the tragedy or feel they were too self-involved and not supportive enough. There is tremendous shame that batters the family, because suicide is unacceptable and frowned upon in Western society.

> "I grew up in a conservative, upper-middle-class neighborhood. I was 10 when my mother suicided," said Eve. "No one talked about it. But I always had the sense that people were disapproving of me. Sometimes at the club I would get a little paranoid when I was introduced to someone new. I'd fantasize that people were talking about me. 'She's the girl whose mother committed suicide.' I felt so ashamed. It's something I carry with me, that terrible shame. When people talk about their mothers, I never say how my mother died. It's such a stigma."

> Paul's father committed suicide when Paul was 18. Paul found him slumped over the steering wheel of the car. Paul's parents were going through a divorce, and his father had recently learned that his wife had begun a new relationship. Paul was furious at his mother, believing she had triggered the father's suicide. His siblings had different reactions. One withdrew, isolated himself, and refused to talk about it; a much younger brother became overtly aggressive and destructive; another brother blamed the father for ruining his life; a sister blamed herself, feeling a sense of responsibility. Each one felt a sense of blame, believing that they somehow could have prevented it.

> Dana said, "I finally met someone who truly understands what it's like not to have a mother. People are always saying to me 'I know how you

must feel' and they don't, how could they? But Joan was also 19 when her mother died, also in college, and also not yet married. A 19-year-old girl without a mother is alone and not like any of her friends. Joan knew this feeling ... much, much later she told me her mother had committed suicide ... she didn't tell me for a long time, she said she felt such shame. Joan told me 'I don't think a day passes that I do not feel the utter loss and loneliness from my mother's suicide ... it haunts me. She committed suicide in the hospital by hanging herself. My guilt lingers for not doing something ... they say time is a great healer, but it never erases the depth of the loss and the longing for her presence. When you lose your mother, nobody can replace her, not a best friend, not a sister, not a husband.'"

"I was nine years old when my mother committed suicide. I remember the phone ringing. I had just come home. My grandmother picked up the phone, and turned to me and said, 'She committed suicide.' It didn't surprise me ... I had an intuitive feeling. She'd been in the hospital for a week for depression ... I remember a couple of months prior to the hospitalization her not being able to get out of bed. ... My father remarried six months later. He married someone from our church. In retrospect, I think they were having an affair. I've always wondered if that's what made my mother so depressed. ... My mother killed herself by putting a plastic garbage-can liner over her head. Years later, I went back to look at the hospital records, which required an endless bureaucratic paper chase. My brother and I are both so angry at our father and stepmother. It seems they maneuvered my mother's death. ... My father never talked to us at all about my mother's death. There was no communication. I knew never to bring my mother up. ... In some ways nothing changed. When Mae moved in, I felt really awful. My father never protected me, she yelled all the time, and did vicious things to me. I've always resented him. I feel I need security, I can't count on anybody or anything because of my mother's death," said Frankie.

In an attempt to cope with the loss, a child may form a pathological identification with the dead parent. For instance, a child may take on a characteristic of the deceased parent in an attempt to be like the deceased parent. The child may develop a high pitched giggle, a raspy voice, a habit of finger-tapping. This pathological identification can result in the child becoming suicidal. Such behavior should immediately be brought to the attention of a child psychiatrist.

Amy Tan,[2] the noted novelist, describes her mother's suicidal identification with her own mother, Tan's grandmother. Tan's mother was only nine when she saw her mother kill herself. Tan describes how, thereafter, some part of her mother remained that nine-year-old who believed that the only escape from any kind of unhappiness was the route her mother took—suicide.

Signs of Suicidal Feelings in Children

1. A child may exhibit prolonged symptoms of grief, including a wish to join the parent—"I don't care that I keep falling off my bike. I don't care if I die, that way I'll be with Dad."

2. Believing that the surviving parent was responsible for the suicide, a child may threaten suicide to punish this parent.

3. A child may have extreme guilt. The child may wish to die to relieve tremendous feelings of guilt that they somehow contributed to their parent's suicide.

4. There may be persistent signs of self-hatred. "I'm too fat/too thin/ too ugly/too stupid. . . ."

5. A child may exhibit persistent feelings of hopelessness.

6. A child may exhibit persistent reckless behavior.

7. Adults may see a preoccupation with death, illustrated in young children by their drawings or play, and in adolescents by giving valued objects away.

8. A child may choose social isolation: wanting to be alone, not wanting to go out, not wanting to participate in social activities that were previously enjoyed.

9. A child may experience recurrent, violent, or self-destructive dreams.

Unexpected, Untimely Deaths

Perhaps the most difficult deaths for children to understand and deal with are those that occur unexpectedly and suddenly. Examples include deaths from violence: plane, auto or train crashes; accidents; war; sudden overwhelming illness, such as heart attacks, or strokes; sniper shootings; bombings; fires; and terrorism. Unexpected, untimely deaths do not allow children any anticipation or preparation. They not only have to deal with the shock but also the loss.

Hank, an attractive and charming 40-year-old man, sought therapy because of problems in his marriage and at work. Hank was 4 years old when his father, a pilot, was shot down and killed in Vietnam. Hank remembers the trauma well. "I remember my mom crying all the time, with silent tears spilling down her cheeks . . . crying while she made dinner, crying when we went to the park and I guess she saw other kids with their dads, crying in church, and, worst of all, at night when she thought I was asleep. I would do anything to make her laugh or smile. And then she met Ed a few years later. He was wonderful to her and to me. Later they married and had two little girls. I always felt they were my family and never felt excluded, but my role was always to try to make people happy no matter what. That got me into a lot of trouble . . . I can't give bad news, I avoid conflict, and I don't always tell the truth. I don't do well with unexpected situations, and even though I've always been proud of my dad, I can't watch war movies."

The largest number of sudden deaths in the United States occurred on September 11, 2001. Thousands of children suddenly lost parents in the vicious attack on the World Trade Center and the Pentagon. Thousands of children were traumatized.

Charlie LeDuff describes this poignantly in a *New York Times* article. "'Mommy, is Daddy dead?' The little boy said it right there at the Burger King. 'Yes, Aidan, Daddy is dead,' said his mother, Marian Fontana. She decided that the raw truth about her husband, Dave, was best. 'Daddy was buried in the rubble of the World Trade Center trying to save people's lives, and died doing something good.' The boy thought for a moment. 'You're a liar,' he decided. 'Daddy's not dead.' So the little boy planned a welcome-home party, and his mother planned a funeral."[3]

"The struggle between denial and acceptance occupies the lives of those left behind by Dave Fontana, one of 12 firefighters from Squad 1 in Park Slope, Brooklyn, who were lost in the attack on the twin towers. It resounds in a wistful 5-year-old son and a heartbreaking practical widow."[4]

On September 11, 2001, an estimated ten thousand children lost a parent. Four-year-old Alexandra Litgay was one of them.

"On September 11 at 9 A.M., Zhanetta Tsoy's life was to begin anew. It was Day 1 of a new job in a new country, a place where she and her husband believed their futures were as big and bright as the New York skyline. Fresh from Kazakhstan, Ms. Tsoy, 32, could hardly believe she was about to go to work in one of the world's tallest buildings as an accountant for Marsh & McLennan. She was so excited that, shortly after arriving in America, on August 23, Ms. Tsoy dragged her husband and 4-year-old daughter on a sightseeing trip to the World Trade Center. Her husband, Vyacheslav Litgay, said she was very hurried when she left for her first morning of work. 'She was afraid that she can't be late,' he said.

'Zhanetta wanted very much to make a good start.' In the days since the towers collapsed, Alexandra's father, Vyacheslav Litgay, has looked for the words to explain the disaster and her mother's death to their daughter. He has searched for the photos of their trip to the trade center, but they have also disappeared. Family members want him and Alexandra to come home to Kazakhstan. Mr. Litgay cannot. 'Dead or alive, this is where my wife is,' he said. 'As long as we are here, she is with us.'"[5]

Although the surviving parent is in shock him- or herself, once calm, the parent needs to sit down quietly with the children, and break the news slowly. The children need time to digest and process the information. If a parent feels too distraught, another close, loving, family member or friend can substitute for the parent. For example, "I have something very upsetting to tell you. This is very sad and painful news. Remember when the phone rang a little while ago, and you knew I was terribly upset? There has been a terrible accident. Mommy (Daddy) was in an accident (bomb, fire). She (he) died."

Euphemisms are confusing. Simple, concrete statements are best. "After her father died on September 11, adults kept telling Samantha Walker, four, that her daddy, Benjamin James Walker, would always be in her heart. She said, 'I don't want Daddy to be in my heart. I want Daddy to be in my house.'"[6]

Another heartrending vignette reported in the *New York Times* describes two little girls whose father never returned home from work. The two little girls were traumatized. They now pepper their mother with questions and express tremendous anxiety over her safety. "If Mommy dies while shopping at Target how will we get home?"[7] The little girls' agony is expressed by their obsession with the song "Please Don't Go."

The intense media coverage surrounding September 11, 2001, was intensely troubling to the surviving parents and children. Watching planes crash into buildings, seeing the fireball, seeing people jump to their deaths, seeing the buildings melt, and knowing that their parents worked in those buildings are unbearable images for any child.

A 14-year-old boy who lost a parent on September 11, 2001, commented on the media coverage. "Learning so much about the subject," he said, "made me feel . . . terrified."

Nightmares, rage, suicidal fantasies, regressive behavior such as bedwetting, fighting with other children, and tremendous anxiety are all manifestations of trauma and the media blitz. These symptoms could persist for years unless addressed in treatment.

Religion helped comfort some survivors.

Enid Marie, age eight, lost her mother on 9/11. She talked to a reporter about her mother's past ministry to children using songs, prayers, and Bible stories. Hymns were her mother's comfort and now have become hers. At the end of the interview Enid started humming "I'm running to the mercy seat where Jesus is calling."

Sonia Ortiz who died in the World Trade Center was convinced of the existence of God and an afterlife. Her daughter said her mother always said she wanted to be up there with her deceased son. "If there's any comfort, it's knowing that she's with him now."

Nick Chirls, age 16, delivered the eulogy for his mother. "As Nick said the word 'mother' . . . the bird lighted upon his head with hundreds of mourners gasping the boy took the bird in his hand then set it free. 'I'm not a religious person' he said later. 'I don't believe in things like that. But there is no other explanation than my mother was with me.'"[8]

Other family members of victims found comfort in nature. Lars Qualben had transformed urban blight into a backyard of trees for his sons when they were toddlers. Now the sons, 15 and 14, find solace for their pain under his trees. "We feel him in our lives by being there. . . . It's a place where he is a living presence."[9]

The memory of a dead parent can be kept alive through stories, mementos, photos, and personal items. These items are essential to help a child through the mourning process.

Gabriella, who is five, wants to know everything about her father. "Did Daddy stay up late after I fell asleep? What was his favorite color? Would he have liked the song playing on the radio now?" Out of memories, children can develop identification with a dead parent.

"Squad 128 was one of the first on the scene on September 11 and lost all seven men, but Lieutenant McGinn has already passed on the firefighting itch. For the past two years, a kid from Staten Island named Sean Bradley spent much of his spare time hanging around Squad 128, where his uncle Billy was a lieutenant. Now Sean, 17, has decided that he wants to be a firefighter, too."[10]

The space program and the nation have suffered several tragedies: the explosions of Apollo I, Challenger, and Columbia. In all instances, there were children who lost parents. These children found comfort knowing their parents became part of a legacy. In the words of June Scobee Rodgers, "Although we grieve deeply, as do the families of Apollo I and Challenger before us, the bold exploration of space must go on . . . the legacy of Columbia must carry on for the benefit of our children and yours."[11]

The Columbia accident left 12 children without parents. "Thirteen men and women know what is in store for the Columbia children as they cope with the loss of their fathers and mothers . . . For the children of the Challenger astronauts, private grief was twisted into public torture. Kathie Scobee Fulgham, daughter of Challenger commander Dick Scobee, wrote in an open letter to the children who lost parents in the September 11 terrorist attacks, "My father died a hundred times a day on television all across the county. . . . The Challenger explosion was a national tragedy. Everyone saw it, everyone hurt, everyone grieved, everyone wanted to help. But that did not make it any easier for me. They wanted to say good-bye to American heroes. I just wanted to say good-bye to my Daddy.'"[12]

Frequently Asked Questions

Three to Five Years

Question: "What will happen to her?"

Answer: "She'll be in Heaven with the angels and grandma and grandpa."

Question: "Can I see Mommy again?"

Answer: "I think she would like you to remember her as she was."

Six to Nine Years

Question: "Why did Mom kill herself? How could she have left me?"

Answer: "Your mother did love you. She was very troubled and wasn't rational. It was an act of desperation."

Question: "Why didn't the doctor help Dad?"

Answer: "He did try to help, but sometimes doctors aren't successful. Dad had a sickness of the mind."

Question: "Mom wasn't sick. Why did she die?"

Answer: "You're right. She wasn't physically sick, but she was very, very troubled and felt no one could help her. Because of the way she was feeling, she took her own life. It's very sad. There was help for her."

Ten to Twelve Years

Question: "Why did she punish us by killing herself?"

Answer: "You're right. It feels like a punishment. But I'm sure that's not what she wanted to do. She was so despairing and so upset. It was irrational, and she was feeling depressed and desperate. But you must remember she loved you very much."

Question: "I guess I wasn't a good enough child; otherwise why would she have left me?"

Answer: "You are a good enough kid. Mom always said so. Mom didn't leave because of you. You're not to blame. It wasn't your fault. It wasn't anyone's fault. Your Mom loved you very much."

Question: "Will I always remember the TV pictures?"

Answer: "I hope you will remember Dad as a scientist who loved the exploration of space. He was a man whose legacy is as a brave astronaut."

Question: "Do you think Dad saw the grenade coming at him?"

Answer: "You need to remember that your Dad was incredibly brave and fighting for freedom. He probably died within seconds, before he had time to register that the grenade would kill him."

Twelve to Eighteen Years

Question: "How can I tell my friends? I'm so embarrassed."

Answer: "Tell your friends your mother was very troubled and that she died."

Question: "Will I die the same way?"

Answer: "If you feel so badly and hopeless, know that there are people and medication that can help. You must ask for help. People don't always know that someone is suffering badly."

CHAPTER 7

THE FIRST ANNIVERSARY

Reactions to the Anniversary of the Death

By the time of the first anniversary, children have an understanding that someone has died; faced the psychological pain of the loss; coped with pain; started to invest in new relationships; developed a new sense of identity that includes experience of the loss; reformulated the relationship to the person who is lost; and returned to age appropriate developmental tasks.

Some of the variables that may affect the successful completion of these tasks are the age of the child, the gender of the child, the birth order of the child, the child's understanding of the concept of death, earlier psychological difficulties, the size of the family, the cohesiveness of the family, the coping style of the family, and the family's ability or inability to provide support. Other variables include the surviving parent's level of vulnerability, consistency and structure provided by the surviving parent, the nature of the pre-death relationship between the child and the deceased parent, the child's ability to anticipate the death, the type of death, and the reaction of the surviving parent.

Perhaps one of the most important variables is the age of the child at the time of the death. For example, a preschool child believes that death is reversible and so asks, "When will Mama be coming back?" At the time of the first anniversary, the young child may still not be able to understand the permanence of the loss, or that the deceased parent is not capable of acting or perceiving anything: "Do you think Mommy thinks I look pretty in my new dress?" By contrast, the child of 4 to 6 years understands that death is final; that the dead parent is nonfunctional and that death is universal. The 7- to 11-year-old has a more realistic understanding of the causality of death. Consequently, at the time of the anniversary, children over the age of 5 are able to understand that a parent will not return.

> As the first anniversary drew near Mrs. K. became apprehensive. Her two children, Sally, age three, and Danny, age eight, had begun to exhibit some regressive and emotionally disturbing behavior. Sally had begun to wet her bed, and Danny had begun to bite his nails and have troubling dreams in which he could not save his father from monsters, lightning, and sidewalks that crumbled and sucked him in. Mrs. K. was encouraged to talk to the children at length about their feelings surrounding their father's death and the upcoming anniversary. Mrs. K. reported that after a few weeks the regressive behaviors calmed down. Together the family decided to visit the grave on the anniversary of the death. Initially, at the gravesite, Sally showed little distress until it was time to leave. She then said to her mother, "Can Daddy come home with us now?" Danny, infuriated, screamed, "He's dead! A car hit him. He's dead! He's never coming home!" and then, sobbing, ran out of the cemetery. Mrs. K. was left to comfort a now bereft Sally who repeated over and over again, "Why can't Daddy come home?"

The first anniversary of the parent's death is sometimes experienced as more painful than the actual death. The anniversary brings about the recognition and realization that the parent is never returning. There has been an entire year of awareness, as well as reminder after reminder of the absence. The family has gone through the first birthday, the first New Year's, Thanksgiving, and Christmas. The cycle of the seasons has been experienced without the parent.

> I was getting dressed to go to my aunt's for Thanksgiving when I realized how much I was dreading it. Everyone would be there with their families, all except me, and I would be alone. I dreaded the way they had looked at me the last few times I had seen them. It was as if I could see how they pitied me. I didn't want their pity. I just wanted my mother to be alive. It had been almost a year since she had died and I found that I was missing her more as time went on, not less. (Mary Ann, age 18)

Some religions mark the anniversary of the death with ritual. Some light candles, some erect tombstones, some recite special prayers commemorating the death.

Dad's death, I didn't believe it at first. It was a two-night wake. I couldn't cry at the cemetery. In fact, for months I was kinda numb. It was on my birthday that I first remember crying. That was about five months after he died. By the time of the first anniversary of his death, I was real depressed. The first anniversary was awful. My mom arranged a mass and when they played "Ava Maria" I could not stop shaking, I had to sit down. I still cannot talk about him without my voice breaking, even though he died when I was a sophomore in high school—10 years ago. (Marcy, age 25)

"I linked arms with my sister and I said, 'Stand close to me. I feel so alone.' I knew this day was going to be very hard. The funeral had had little impact on me—it was a blur, and it was a shock. As we stood together, her girls, in front of the cloth-covered tombstone, we both started to cry. And then, the worst moment came: There was her name boldly etched into the marble. It couldn't be! 'Sarah Nicholas, beloved wife and mother of . . . ' No, it couldn't be, I couldn't bear it to be. It was probably the worst moment of my life." (Sandra, age 15)

The first anniversary of the parent's death provokes a host of emotional reactions—sadness, anxiety, and sometimes regression. As we saw with Sandra, it took an entire year for her to begin to feel the impact of the loss. It is, perhaps, for this reason that many religions mark the first anniversary of a death. It enables people to express and come to terms with their emotions.

As the year draws to an end, some of a child's earlier behaviors may resurface: irritability, sadness, anxiety, fatigue, loneliness, restlessness, lack of concentration, yearning, preoccupation, sleep disturbance, bad dreams, absent-mindedness, social withdrawal, treasuring objects belonging to the deceased parent.

"I started crying only about a year after her death, and it seemed as if I never stopped. When I was nine, a friend accidentally shattered one of my mother's precious champagne glasses that she had loved. I was distraught. I actually made quite a scene! I cried, I clutched the glass to my breast and kept saying, 'Oh, no. Oh, no!' Later I realized that my over-reaction was really a statement of my pain." (Katherine, age 19)

In younger children, regression is often evident at the time of the first anniversary. Shelly, a three-year-old, started displaying the behavior of a much younger child. She started to wet her bed again, she reverted to calling her father "Dada," a name she had not used for a couple of years, and she insisted on being carried upstairs to bed each night. Children tend to regress when they are very upset. At these times a parent needs to be patient, reassuring, comforting, and offer as much security as possible.

As the first anniversary approaches, children might attempt to soothe and comfort themselves. Younger children may start thumb sucking or rocking; older children might sleep more, eat more, and watch more television.

> Around the time of the anniversary of his wife's death, Arthur's father was badly startled when he walked into his bedroom and found his deceased wife's chair returned to the center of the room. "I caught my breath. After Lynn's death, I had put away her chair that she had spent the last few months of her life resting in. And there it was back in the middle of the room, empty. It was eerie and unsettling. I later found out that Arthur, age 10, had replicated the scene of his mother's final days. The housekeeper told me that after school he spent hours lying in the chair watching television. Being in his mother's chair seemed to bring comfort to him."

A parent or caregiver needs to be hyper-vigilant around the time of the first anniversary. With emotions escalating, children are sometimes propelled into troubling situations.

> Michael, age 10, had been involved in a series of bike accidents culminating, a week before the anniversary of his father's death, in a severe accident in which he suffered a concussion. Michael's preoccupation was so intense that he was not paying attention to anything around him. After the first accident it would have been helpful had his mother been alert to Michael's emotional state. The concussion might then have been avoided.

It is important for the surviving parent to acknowledge the actual anniversary of the death. Everyone in the family is excruciatingly aware of the upcoming day, and the tendency towards a conspiracy of silence needs to be broken. The first anniversary needs to be noted; it must not be ignored. The surviving parent needs to talk to the children well before the anniversary. Preparing for the anniversary becomes a necessary ritual to anticipate, accept, and acknowledge.

Parents should be aware that successive anniversaries may remain difficult; these days will continue to remind the children of their earlier loss. Although with time there is a gradual acceptance of the terrible loss, the death of a parent is a loss that is eternal.

> But O for the touch of a vanish'd hand,
> And the sound of a voice that is still!
> —Alfred Lord Tennyson

Frequently Asked Questions

Three to Five Years

Question: "Danny said, 'Mommy has been dead for a year.' Can she come home now?"

Answer: "Remember what I told you. Mommy can never come home again. She loved you very much. She's in Heaven now."

Six to Nine Years

Question: "Will I always feel so upset on her anniversary?"

Answer: "You will always be aware of the date. Your feelings may not be as raw, but the day will always be a sad one for you."

Question: "How can I be sure I never forget Daddy? It's only one year and I can't remember his voice anymore."

Answer: "You will never forget Daddy. You have memories and pictures. We will always be talking to each other about Daddy and things we did together. We will never forget him."

Ten to Twelve Years

Question: "I'm so sad today, I wasn't so sad at the funeral."

Answer: "Sometimes it takes a long time for the thoughts and feelings to come together. Sometimes we're in shock, and the feelings are cut off."

Question: "Why do we only put up a tombstone after a year?"

Answer: "Jewish people believe that it takes a full year to mourn—you have to go through birthdays, holidays, and all the seasons without the person in order to fully grieve."

Twelve to Eighteen Years

Question: "I don't want to cry in front of everyone. How can I stop myself?"

Answer: "It's okay to show your feelings. People cry because they have feelings. There is nothing wrong with showing your feelings."

CHAPTER 8

INTERVIEWS

Jane, age 57; Julia, age 54; and Maggie, age 45, are three sisters whose mother died 40 years ago of breast cancer when they were 17, 14, and 5, respectively. Their interviews richly illustrate the profound pain of their loss, and their memories illuminate much of what this book is about. The stories they share bring the book to life and make it very real. We are deeply appreciative.

Jane

Q: Tell us from the beginning. Tell us, you were seventeen?

A: Well, I mean, do you want to go back to when she got sick?

Q: Yes, exactly.

A: I was fourteen when my mother got sick. We moved to Chicago in 1960. And now, again, these are all my memories. They may be so totally different. But we moved here in 1960, and I was a sophomore in high school. And my mother was not very, she didn't want to do anything to rock the boat, as I'm sure you know, but you don't because you've not spoken with my sister Julia. My father was extremely volatile. He was, the slightest thing could set him off. So if somebody was sick or they didn't feel well, you never really said anything because you didn't know if you were going to cause World War III.

So it was a long time I recall from the time she found a lump until she actually went to the doctor. There was something under her left arm as I recall.

Q: Did she share that information with you?

A: No. No, there was absolutely nothing shared. This all came out after she went for a biopsy. And the horror story besides the fact that she had no one to talk to about this was that she didn't take care of this problem until the lump became so painful she couldn't move her arm. Now this was 1960, and cancer was like AIDS then. People didn't talk about anything. I guess she figured it would go away. But I don't know if you are familiar with that horrible place over on Ashland Avenue, the Edgewater Hospital, the old Maizel Hospital. Well, she went there for her biopsy and they sent her home; they said she was fine. And they called, as I remember, about two weeks later, and they said she wasn't fine. They had screwed up the slides in the lab. And that the lymph nodes they had taken had cancer. So they rushed her, and they did a radical mastectomy. Again, none of us were told anything.

Q: What were you told? Why did you think your mom was in the hospital?

A: I don't remember. It's a void. I mean, there's just these blank pieces. The word *cancer* was never mentioned, ever in our house. She came home, she wasn't doing well. I remember her going to the University of Chicago, I think it was every day. I don't remember if it was for chemo or for radiation. I don't remember what her course of treatment was. But it knocked her on her ass. It was not good. And my father who was just a peach to start with, I remember him as being totally non-supportive of what she was going through. It was more of an inconvenience to him. Because he had these three kids, and we were like too much for him to handle, and who was going to help him with the kids. And when she finally got so sick that they put her in Grant Hospital—here's a little symmetry. Grant was where I was born, where both of my children were born, and where my mother died. So there's a lot of history at that one hospital (cries).

They told my mother she had something called *neuralgia*, which was why she was in all this pain. And they used to pump her up with morphine, but it was only every four hours, because, God forbid, you should become addicted while you're dying. It's just a wonderful . . . doesn't it make you furious? And I remember my mother's parents, my grandparents, sitting in that hallway day after day, crying and crying and crying. And my father was raging up and down the hall looking for someone to get angry with. His brother—my father is the youngest of three boys—my Uncle Leo, came in from California, and I don't know what my father thought he could do, but he thought that Leo could make things all better, and Leo couldn't make things all better.

Q: What was your understanding of what was happening?

A: Well, you know, I knew she was dying. But nobody knew from what really. I mean, I think there might have been, I might have overheard my grandparents or my aunts or my uncles saying something about cancer or breast cancer. I don't remember. But I just remember that I would get off that elevator on the floor at Grant and I would hear her screaming from the pain down the hall because it wasn't time for her to have her medication. And that's what I remember.

Q: That's a terrible memory. And you were young. What could you do?

A: And you felt, or I felt, as a kid that there was absolutely no comfort, no one to turn to because my father was so emotionally unavailable before my mother got sick. So out of his mind when all of this was going on that there was just, there was no shelter in the storm, there was no port in the storm (cries hard).

Q: So could you talk to nobody? And you were the oldest? There was no one.

A: It was a horrible, I mean, I think the oldest kids always get it worse anyway. I mean, I have two kids, and I know I was much rougher on my son than my daughter. Because you learn how to parent with your first child. It's just the way things happen. But my father was such a physically abusive person and such a verbally abusive person. And his way of making himself feel better was making everybody else feel bad that you really didn't want to go there. And we were not, if my memory is correct, we were not at the hospital when my mother died that particular afternoon. I think I was at home. My dad was at the hospital. And I think my mother's brother and my aunt and my grandparents were there, I think. You know, it's 30 years this year. September will be thirty years (cries).

Q: It still hurts.

A: Well, I took it as far as I could take it. I've been in and out of therapy about this for a long time. And you know you work on a piece, and at least for me, I work on a piece, and then I stop, and then I work on another piece. And I went as far as I could with a lot of this, and a lot of it still isn't finished. I don't think it's ever finished (cries).

Q: Who told you that your mother had died?

A: My uncle, my mom's brother, I think. And I remember we lived in an apartment at Peterson Park. We lived at Washtenaw and California. And everybody came back from the hospital, and I remember making dinner. And we sat around this tiny table in the kitchen, and everybody was numb, everybody was just numb. And then the next thing I remember, we were at Weinstein's for the funeral. And then we were sitting shivah for a week. And then everybody went away and left us with this maniac.

Q: Do you remember the funeral?

A: Not really. No.

Q: Do you remember how your uncle told you your mother died?

A: No. No. There were a lot of things going on. First of all, my mother's family from the time my parents got together never liked my dad. So you had all of this going on. So there was all of this stuff. And I don't know if, consciously or unconsciously, my mother's family blamed my father for my mother getting sick, not getting the right care. But there was, besides the grieving, there was a lot of anger. And I saw the adults around me being very conflicted about what they were trying to do. So they were trying to sort out their own stuff. I can't even tell you what was going on with Julia and Maggie at that time. I mean, I was in such a turmoil.

I was 17. I graduated high school in June of '63, and my mother passed away in September of '63. I had gotten a par-tial scholarship to the Art Institute. My father informed me that I wasn't going to go. I was going to stay home and take care of my sisters. So I was out of the house and married at 19.

I mean, the man was nuts. I had to get out of the house. I found someone who was the antithesis of who he was. The marriage lasted for 7, 8 years. It wasn't a long marriage, but it got me out of that house. I was 19. I mean, who the hell knew what you want to do when you're 19 years old? But it got me out of the house. And then my father, just a little over a year after my mother died, remarried.

Q: Wait, wait. Don't rush ahead. I want to go back.

A: No, but I'm trying to put things in chronological order. So I was home with Julia and Maggie for just two years. So all I really had was two years. And I remember after my mom died, we closed up that apartment. And what I remember is that there were some small things, of my mother's that my father gave us. I think Julia has my mother's watch. And I don't know how it came to me, but I had my mother's wedding ring and engagement ring; it came to me. And that's all I remember. And I have a small little carving that was hers. But you know, nobody said do you want anything, do you want to go through your mom's stuff. It was just the stuff was gone (cries).

Q: How quickly was it gone?

A: I would say within a week after the funeral.

Q: Were there photographs around the place?

A: Years later I got a couple of photo albums from my mom's sisters in California, and they were pictures from when I was very small and when Julia was a baby. Anything that was in the house that was personal, I don't remember that being offered to any of us. I don't know, I don't even remember when we moved to a different apartment, if any of the furniture from the apartment that we were in when my mother died came with us. Like I say, there are these huge big blank walls I can't recall.

Q: But you do remember everything was just boxed up and gone.

A: I went to school one day, and I think my father had like the Council for the Jewish Elderly or the ARK or one of the Jewish agencies come while we were at school and take all of her clothes. And I remember my aunt picking out a suit, a blue suit that she wore when she was buried. No, I don't remember what happened to her other clothes. I remember that last year of her life she was scared to death, looking back on it now. I mean, then I didn't know what it was. I think she knew she was dying. And she couldn't say anything. So it was horrible (tearful).

Q: What were the first few months like? You moved pretty soon.

A: I think within a matter of months we moved. It was the same neighborhood. Julia and Maggie stayed at the same schools. I was going to the Pier at the time.

Q: Oh, he let you go to college? He wouldn't let you go to the Art Institute?

A: No, but I had one semester at the Pier. And Julia was in high school and Maggie was, I don't even remember, she was five. Who took care of her during the day? See, I can't recall who did that.

Q: Maybe you did because you were finished with high school. And that's why your dad didn't let you go to the Art Institute.

A: I can't remember. I just can't remember. But I think my grandparents still lived in Chicago and had not moved to California. And these are my mom's parents. And if they did, they were close, and they may have taken her during the day. Oh, no. OK. She was in nursery school. That's where she was at. She was in a preschool in Rogers Park. Where was she after school? I think by the time they brought her home, I was home, Julia was home.

Q: Did you do the cooking and laundry?

A: Yeah. My father wanted to make sure his life was ordered. It's all about order. It took me years to figure out that he was nuts because my grandparents were more than a little whacked out. But he would pull some stuff that was just amazing. So it was nobody ever came to the house. My friends wouldn't come because they never knew when there was going to be an explosion with him, and they just didn't want to get involved. My best friend from high school lived down the street. And her parents were very kind. They had their own stuff. Her parents were Holocaust survivors. And her dad worked nights, and so I would walk down the street to Jeanie's house, and her mother would be home, and I remember I would walk down there with Maggie, and we would sit sometime in the afternoon.

But I remember my mother being pretty isolated. Her whole world was in California. When we moved back here, it's like she really didn't have anybody. And to this day I can't tell you why we moved back here. That was another one of the family's big secrets. We moved back when I was 14, and I had no idea why. But the house was sold in California and we came back and that was it. And shortly after that, we came back in '60, so it might have been '60 or '61 that she got ill.

Q: Jane, then when did he remarry? How much later?

A: It was I would say not more than a year and a half after my mom died.

Q: And how were you told about this?

A: Oh, God. He met this woman through a cousin. And she was divorced with two small kids who were, Louise was a year older than Maggie and Tom was a year older than Louise. So there was a stepbrother and stepsister much younger than me. And my cousin introduced them, and my father took us, and I know Julia went with me, but I don't remember if Maggie was there. But we went to a restaurant downtown and met her for dinner. And I just couldn't stand her from the minute that I met her for a lot of different reasons. I think a lot of it wasn't her fault. I think she was just sort of thrown at us. But I was 18 years old, and what the hell did I know.

Q: Your mother had just died.

A: And she was only 10 years older than I was. And she made it quite clear after—and I don't want to jump ahead—but I mean, I just picked up the energy from her that was just not warm and fuzzy, and she was really looking for somebody who would take care of her and her kids. And that's what I picked up from her. And I just didn't like her. So I just kept my distance. And Julia tried to get along. Julia has always been, she always wants to get along with everybody. I love her to death, but sometimes it just ain't there.

Q: When you went down to meet this woman for dinner, were you told why you were going downtown for dinner?

A: Not until we were at the table. And then my father said that this was Katrina, and they were going to get married.

Q: There was no preparation at all.

A: No, because we were never told anything. I mean, it all falls into a pattern if you really think about it. My mother never told us when she got sick. We were never really told why she was sick. Nothing was ever discussed while she was dying, so why should we be told anything now? It was definitely a time where kids were seen and not heard. And I was always getting into trouble, because my attitude was, well, I have a right to know. So I would always ask the questions that would cause a big explosion, and I really didn't care.

Q: Were you able to talk at all to your father before he married, about your mother, like with any reminiscing or-. . . . ?

A: He wouldn't talk about her. The only one memory I have maybe because she died around Labor Day, so I remembered something pretty warm, and the windows being open at night. The layout of the apartment, Julia and I shared a bedroom, and then there was a bathroom, and my parents' room where my father was. And then there was a closed-in porch, I'm sure you'll remember, like in some of the old apartments, and that was Maggie's room. But my father would pace the floors at two o'clock in the morning, carrying my mother's picture around, screaming at her how could she die and leave him with three kids. He was a mess. He was an absolute mess, and he wasn't, as far as I know, trying to do anything to process his feelings, and he certainly wasn't doing anything to help us work on ours. And he really took this whole thing as a personal affront from the universe. This was done by the gods simply to piss him off and make his life difficult. And I'm looking at this guy and I'm going, "You are really not there, you are just not getting this."

 I don't remember really too much of what went on in that house, except it was extremely tense. The slightest thing could cause a huge explosion. It was almost like being in boot camp. He had his rules about how that house needed be run, and if they weren't run that way you paid the price. But nobody ever talked about it. Maggie was too little. Julia didn't want to make waves. And I would go down the street to my friend Jeanie's. I said, "I don't want to deal with this."

Q: And then when you were introduced to Kat and told he was going to marry her . . . at the dinner table. What did the three of you do?

A: I think we just looked at each other. Didn't say anything. Sort of like he made up his mind, this is what he's going to do. And I had pretty much decided by that point, because a year had passed, and Ken and I had been going out since I was like a junior in high school. And his parents were wonderful. They were terrific. My father couldn't stand him because he was Catholic. So I mean, how much now going back on it did I marry a Catholic just to piss my father off? Probably a huge amount. But, at the time, I was just looking at the point that I needed to get out of there. And the kindness that his parents showed me I had never seen in my own home. So I figured, OK, he's safe.

Q: And he wasn't volatile.

A: No. This was a nice Polish Catholic boy from the southwest side. Poor thing, he had no clue either, no clue. And when I told my dad that we were getting married, he went crazy. "You can't marry that Polack." I said, "Well, I can do whatever I want. I'm 18, you can't tell me what to do."

Q: He was already married, your dad?

A: No. Ken and I got married in January of 1965, because my son was born in December of '65, and I think my father got married in March of 1965. So maybe my dad got married a year and a half after my mother died. She died in September of '63. I never really sat and thought about the time. So September of '63 to March of '65 is what? About 18 months? Because that's what I'm remembering.

Q: Do you remember Kat coming into the household?

A: No, because I was gone.

Q: What about holidays like Passover or all the Jewish holidays or Thanksgiving? What were those like?

A: Birthdays, when my mother was sick, before she got sick?

Q: After she got sick.

A: The last thing I recall her doing was making a graduation party for me from high school. I think we went to my grandparents for the Jewish holiday. They lived up on Devon Avenue. Or to my Uncle Alex, my mother's brother, on the Jewish holidays. Occasionally we would have people to our house, but people didn't like to come to our house, because inevitably there would be, my father would throw a fit of some kind for whatever reason. Somebody would have affronted him or not treated him right. I mean, it was like he was always looking for a reason to pick a fight with someone. So no, I don't recall.

Q: And after she died, Jane, what about the holidays? What were they like without her?

A: Well, I don't recall there being anything.

Q: There was no celebrations?

A: Not that I remember. That doesn't mean there wasn't.

Q: She died in September, so I'm thinking the first holiday after could have been Rosh Hashanah, or it could have been Thanksgiving.

A: Not a clue. Oh, I do remember. We moved to the new apartment and I remember we had my aunt and uncle over for Thanksgiving dinner and I made Thanksgiving dinner. And I had always cooked with a gas stove. Well, we had an electric stove in this new apartment. I had no clue. So I cooked the turkey, and the turkey wasn't cooked. And my father had the best time making fun of the fact that I didn't know what I was doing, and what an idiot I was. So then I just gave up.

Q: Tell us about your son being born.

A: He was born on my twentieth birthday. Yeah, there's a little comic retribution. I mean, my father didn't talk to me for the whole first year I got married. And then I mean just to nudge just a little bit, I made sure we had him baptized. But my dad came over because he finally had a grandchild. I didn't see my father from the time I told him I was getting married. He forbid my sisters to come to my wedding. He wouldn't let them come. And we got married in Ken's parish on the south side, and his parents threw us a very nice party. And it's like my whole life up here was over because I couldn't see my sisters. They were kids, and they couldn't come. He wouldn't let Julia or Maggie come. But when Jordan was born, he suddenly had a grandson, and he wanted back in my life. And the first time I saw my father after I had gotten married was in December. I'm in labor. OK, now I want to deal with this? And he walks into the hospital at Grant, and he walks in and he says, "I'm Dr. Silverman, and I'm here to see my daughter." And I had a fit. I said, "Get him out of here." "How can you talk to me like this? "I'm your father." I said, "You are nothing to me." It was not pretty. I remember I threw a tray of instruments at him. And then I didn't see him until my son's christening. You laugh now, but at the time, I'm 20 years old and I'm. . . . oh, my God.

Q: It must have been awful for you, though, because to think that your mother died in September, your birthday is in December. That must have been very hard for you. What was that first year like?

A: I don't remember. I was at the Pier. I went there one semester and then . . . and I don't think I went that first year my mother died. I think I might have gone in January of '64. I think. . . .

Q: What advice would you give parents?

A: I think as hard as it is to process your own pain, you cannot use your kids as your whipping post while you're trying to figure out what you're doing. You can't make them responsible for the death of your partner. You can't make the kids feel that it's their fault. And that's how I felt (cries).

Q: So you felt by your father's constant anger that he was making the three of you feel responsible for what had happened?

A: Well, his anger, his lack of communication, his terror; he was terrified. I mean, if I think back on this now, he was 39 years old with three children. My mother was 39 when she died. And I was convinced—now again, I can laugh at this because I'm way past 39, but I was convinced I was never going to make it to 40. And the day of my fortieth birthday, my friend Elizabeth (sick woman that she is) sends a huge funeral wreath to me at my office with this big ribbon across it that said "See, you made it." And it was like I could breathe again. And Julia and I have talked about this, about 6 months before I turned 39, I started feeling I was not going to see 40. And Julia poo-pooed it; she goes, "Ah, you know you're overreacting." Well, guess what happened to her? Hello, same thing. She wasn't as vocal about it, because I kvetch a lot more than she does. But it's very weird.

Now my dad died at 59. I was just 57 this year. And he died of a heart attack at 59. And a year ago, August, I had a triple bypass. I was convinced that I was going to get breast cancer and die like my mother at 39, never thinking about all the other bad genetics on my dad's side of the family. And what did I end up with? His diabetes, his high cholesterol, and his heart disease.

Q: Do you remember ever visiting your mom's grave?

A: I used to go right after she died. I would sit there, and I would yell at her. And I would say, "How could you leave me with this idiot?" I said, "You know he's crazy. How could you leave us there?" And I was very, very angry. I was so angry with my mother before I started seeing Sylvia (therapist), before I started seeing Ruth (therapist), I stopped going. And I don't think I've been to my mom's grave in 20 years. And I've never been to my father's.

Q: But you did go before. You married at 19, so that means that after she died you did go.

A: I did go, yeah. I went a few times the first couple of years. And I felt I got nothing from it. I was very unmoved, and I really didn't want to think of my mother in that grave. So, I mean, for some people it's very much a ritualistic healing, and going to a cemetery helps them move on. But it never did anything for me.

Q: What about the stone setting which you did about a year later? Do you remember that?

A: Not really. Not really. I just was pretty out of it. I was very shut down emotionally, and I don't really think I got my life back until I was 35. That to me was the year that I started working with Ruth Siegel (therapist) and I really started to reclaim some of the things that had just been pushed down for so long.

Q: But that would have been about the age that your mother was when she got sick, wasn't it?

A: She was about 36, 37.

Q: Or do you think it was more that you met someone who you really could work with, Ms. Siegel?

A: Well, there was trust. And it's very interesting, my partner is an only child, and when her mom had her she almost died. It was a very rough delivery so she could never have more kids. We've been together for 6 years. She has bonded with Julia and Maggie. She has a sister she never had. Her mother is like the mother I never got to have. Now, her mom, if my mom were alive I think she'd be 80 this year, so Gail's mother is going to be 83 in October. So I told Gail it was a great trade. I got a mom, and she got two sisters, and it's wonderful. Sometimes you don't always get what you want, but you always end up getting what you need.

Q: You've been incredibly helpful, incredibly open. What would you like to be named in the book?

A: Jane. That's Gail's mother's name.

Q: Is there anything else you would like to tell us?

A: Gail's mother and aunt had a hard time when the aunt got ill. She had a very hard time being sick; she didn't deal with the fact that she was sick very well, so she was very nasty to a lot of people around her. And it would upset Gail's mother. Those two broads were a trip together. They were like, I used to call them the tap dancing sisters. They were fabulous. When I met Gail's mom, Helen was the older by three years. So the difference between her and Gail's mother was the same as between Julia and I. And I just see Julia in myself. And Aunt Helen always had on her little gold shoes and her handbag, and she was wonderful, just the best.

And so then I started talking about my mom and all this stuff to Gail's mother, and I saw the dynamics between the sisters change a little bit. So Gail said I put the whole family in therapy. And I said, "You know, it's not the worst thing that you talk about this stuff." After that I would see that things were working a little bit better. Things that Helen would say to Jane would not get Jane so nuts. Jane would come back and sit down and say, "I have to talk to you," and I would go, "OK. Tell me what's going on." Talking always helps.

And Gail used to say, "You can't be nice to me, you can't be nice to Mom." I said, "Why?" "Because we'll cry." I said, "Well get over it; cry." So you learn from the people around you that you love. And I think, more than anything, you have to allow people to feel. And I don't know if it was being of a certain time or a certain place or what it was, but nobody was allowed to be in touch with anything at that time. So culturally, I'm hoping that things are different now.

Q: I think they are.

A: Well, nobody talked about it when I was a young girl, because nobody wanted to get my father on a tangent.

Julia

Q: We'd like to know all the stories. Tell us when you first discovered that your mother was sick.

A: It's always been, I guess every family has its own survival. Each kid in the family learns what's the best way for him or her to behave. My sister, Jane, who you've met, she had a tougher time than I, or so it seemed, because she was more out there, and my dad was more impatient. So between the two of them, there was a clash. Jane is three years older than I. And I guess I learned at a very young age that if I just am compliant that people won't mess with you so much. So, I mean, I learned very early to be a caregiver and to be the smiling one, and I was really low maintenance. But I think before I reduce myself to nothing, I was a pretty happy kid though. I had friends, and I liked school, and I liked my family. But I learned that if you're accommodating to people, that in my family that was a safer way to be.

When my mother died I was 14—Jane was 17, I was 14, and Maggie was 5. And when my mom got sick, I was still in eighth grade that year. I think my mom was sick for about a year, year and a half.

When my mother died, and I was 14, of my close friends, nobody had had a major loss. I'm not even sure if people had lost grandparents at that point. I imagine some may have. But nobody had lost a parent. And I'm sure I've shared this with you, but I haven't thought about this, but it kind of strings things together—my girlfriends and some of the boys came to the house for a shivah [condolence call], and they were scared just as I know I would have been, but they were really scared. And, again, I was more concerned about making them comfortable than showing my own grief. Because I think I learned that grief meant maintenance for somebody else and that maybe it meant that I would upset things. So, I mean, I think that that's probably why I just learned over the years, I've learned it well, but it's a bad lesson to know, how to kind of say, "I'll be fine."

And so we were talking about this a couple of weeks ago. . . . And I stopped you mid-sentence and I said "Holy moly," here I am, this kid, and it never crossed my mind to say to my dad "I feel terrible," or "Help me," or "How are we going to get through this?" or "What does this mean for us?" And when you talk to Maggie, you know, poor Maggie, she copes differently. Each of us has found a different coping mechanism. But Maggie was so young. I think one of the scariest things for me, you think as a parent that you're so important in your child's life especially when they're little that there is absolutely no way that you would not be the central memory or the central focus. And I know sometimes our memory saves us from hurt feelings. So I don't know what's going on with Maggie, but Maggie really doesn't have any memories of my mom. She was five years old when my mom passed away (tearful).

In my family, this is a story, I don't know if Maggie will tell it. Jane doesn't know it. But I remember when Maggie was born, because I'm nine years older than she. And I was at a Brownie meeting, and somebody tapped me on the shoulder and said we just heard that your mom had a baby; she had a little girl. Everything is fine. And I was like real excited. And my neighbors took us to dinner that night. When you're nine and have a new baby in the house, this is not sibling rivalry, this is a delight, particularly if you're a female and this new baby is a little girl, too. Oh, my girlfriends thought she was adorable. They didn't mind taking her places. It's not like when your sister is two years younger, and everybody complains. Now every time we have a birthday in my family, I say to Maggie, "I remember the day you were born." And I started to do that actually with my nieces and nephews too.

And I wish people had memories about me. I think that's really what this is about. I have memories to share with Maggie. Nobody has memories of me! But I never asked for very much, so I thought, well, I could save Maggie. I tell her I remember the day you were born, and everybody was happy. So I've done that with her kids on their birthdays too. I say, "I remember the day you were born." And I just turned 54, and my nephew called me, who is 18, and he said to me, "Auntie Julia, I remember the day you were born." So it's kind of a joke in our family now.

But I think, I think I feel this loss mostly when I put myself in my role as a mother. Now it's going to get hard (cries). But you know it's so easy to love your child, even when you want to kill them! It's so easy to love them. When you're recognizing all you're giving and realizing the fact that you didn't have it for very long, it's sad. I was only 14 years old. So I mean I had a lot of good years. My own sister, Maggie, I don't know what she'll tell you, but she only had 5 years with our mother.

I asked Maggie if she would come and do this interview and told her that I was just beginning to understand it. I almost said to you, "Paddy, I don't care what else we talk about, because we could talk a lot about Allen (my son) and his thoughts, but I want to be sure we talk about this thing with me, because there's this gook that I've got to get out." Well, and I said to Maggie, "Paddy said to me 'You know you've been carrying this around for 40 years.'" And you know there's all these studies about men who stuff their feelings, they talk about people stuffing it. I don't like that phrase, but when you and I were talking recently, I thought, "Damn that's what I've been doing. I've carried this for 40 years."

Q: That's always been your way. Because even in talking now, you'll talk a bit about yourself and then you'll go back to "But Maggie was so little, and I was 14." It's always the other person, not you.

A: But for me at the time, that was really the reality of how I saw it. You can't change things. But my sister, Jane, was very high maintenance. But she was sweet. I call her my love sister. And I've got great sisters. I really have wonderful, wonderful sisters. But Jane and I share a history that Maggie and I don't share, simply because it's the difference in our age.

Q: Go back to the very beginning, like when your mom was first sick. Who told you about it? How did you find out?

A: You know, I'm trying to remember. There's a whole chronology. I was born in California, and my sister Jane was born here. And I think my family had moved to California. Then we came back to Chicago. When we moved—this relates to my mom—you know, if you believe the studies about stress and cancer and big life changes and so forth. So she was 34 and had a baby, and, at 37, moved with three kids cross-country away from her family, and my dad started a new career, and she died at 39.

So we came to Chicago. That was the first time in my life I ever knew I was unhappy. I can talk about that. It was really painful. But, in fairness, by winter break, I already had friends and I was invited to sleepovers and going to the movies.

I graduated eighth grade in January of 1963. My mother had already had her first surgery. I think this was kind of like a year from beginning to end, but I don't know all the details. So it would have been January of '63. My mother died in September of '63. And I think in 1962, in the fall of '62, maybe late summer was when she was first ill.

Q: How do you remember being told about that or recognizing that?

A: You know, I'm trying to remember. I knew because I went to visit her in the hospital. I knew it was breast cancer. What I remember is she had a really hard time, I guess, with lymph-node issues, and so her arm was always sore. I remember her crying. I know your question is do I remember being told. You know, I don't.

Q: Do you remember seeing her in the hospital? What do you remember?

A: Yeah. But, see, when she was first sick, when they first did the mastectomy and she came home, that wasn't full of hospital visits. I mean there were hospital visits where my dad and my older sister would go. And Maggie was so little at that time. I mean Maggie wasn't part of any of this time. Somebody always stayed with Maggie. But the following summer when she got sick again, and I don't really know, I can't tell you about the year in between except that she was very uncomfortable. But my recollection is that she went into the hospital. So this is January when I graduated grammar school, and she was at that graduation, and she had been fitted for prosthesis, and she was trying to be part of life. She was really trying to be part of life and care for her family. But, by summertime, she was sick or uncomfortable or whatever, and she was back in the hospital for most of the summer. I did a summer-school class, and I would go to summer school from like 8:00 A.M. until 11:30 A.M. or 12:00 P.M. And I went to Mather High School, and my mom was at Grant Hospital, so I would take the Lincoln Avenue bus, which was right in front of the school, and it would drop me right off at the hospital. And I went every day.

Q: But what do you remember about going to the hospital and how it made you feel and how you experienced that?

A: Well, you know it was too typical of me. It was "I'm going to be okay." I don't know what Jane said to you, but I don't remember conversations with her, and if there was anybody I was going to really feel free enough to say this to, it would have been Jane. I don't remember the two of us talking about this, crying about it, worrying about it. My emotional response often came when my dad would come home, and he would be really sad, and he would be really scared, and my need to comfort him. And, actually, when I think about it, I was probably, it gave me an opportunity to cry and comfort myself without using the words. You know, because here was this form, here was this man who was crying, and I felt then that I could cry too. And I could say, "This is really sad," you know. But I think, as a kid, I guess, of that generation or in my family, I wasn't comfortable asking too many questions. And I'm not sure my dad wanted to deal with the truth very well, either. You know, I mean everybody wants to hang on to this possibility of hope.

So I went to the hospital, and then, come late August, my mom got really sick. And this freaks me out (cries hard). A couple of days before my mother died, she died on September the fourth, and it was my first day of high school in the real building, because that first semester I was at kind of like a satellite site, and I had gone to school the first day and found out that she passed away. But I had known for the prior three or four or five days that it wasn't looking good. But this was my first experience. My Uncle Leo, the urologist, came in from California. My mother has two sisters; they were here. My grandmother, too. I mean, can you imagine losing a child?

So here's my grandma, and my mother was so young. All of that stuff, too, when you're young. Who knows how young 39 is. I mean, there's so many parts of it. There's so many parts to this that I can tell you in facts, but I can't tell you from my heart. This is sad (very tearful).

My uncle came to town, and I was too young to be part of this, but what do you do? Do you let someone suffer, or do you stop the treatment and give this person peace and let them die? And I remember hearing that conversation.

Q: Were you a part of the conversation?

A: Yeah, but I wasn't a part of the conversation with my uncle. I think my father and uncle had had the conversation and that my dad was really angry, but he knew my uncle was right, because my uncle had pretty much said, "Alfred, this is not going to get better." And at this point, and I don't really know what the final analysis of her disease, the final diagnosis was, but I was always led to believe that there was something that had gone to the brain. In the last couple of days, my mom was in a coma. Prior to that, when I would go to see her in the hospital, we would always talk. Some days she looked better than others, but she never looked scary to me. It wasn't, maybe it should have been, it probably was. What the hell do I know? I went, and I was glad to go. And I always told her things were fine, and Maggie was good, and we were fine, because I didn't want to say to her I was sad or scared, and I didn't know what I was feeling. I mean, how the hell can you be that age and have your mother dying and be fine? You can't. You can't be fine. And nobody said to me, "You don't have to be strong." And no one even said to me, "You are strong." But nobody said to me, "You don't have to be strong."

I had a girlfriend at the time, Leslie Zimmerman, who was very, very loving to me. It freaked her out that my mother was in the hospital. But I didn't want to go there, I guess. I didn't want to deal with that. Anyway, my dad came home when my uncle was in town and was talking about Leo having said that maybe this suffering should stop. And I do remember, I don't remember saying it out loud, but I remember feeling it, because I've told other people this. I didn't understand how suffering had anything to do with this. I wanted my mother to be alive (cries). I don't think I spoke those words to my father. I doubt that I did, because that would have been quite a statement to make.

But, over the weekend, I was in the hospital, and she was in intensive care, and the visitation at that time was ten minutes on the hour. And I went into that room alone. I swear to God, this has got to be a real memory. Did you ever have issues with memories, and you can't remember if it really happened or if someone told you? But this is my memory. That I went into that room. I don't know where Jane was. My mother woke up or she didn't wake up, but she started to talk. And she said to me, "Julia, I'm going to die, aren't I?" And I don't know what I said. I want to think I said "No, you're not." But she said, "I'm going to die." She said it again. And I walked out of that room and I never told anybody until a few years later (cries). And when I told my dad, he cried so hard. To this day, I love my father, but I don't know if he was crying over the situation or the fact that I had been put in that situation. As a parent myself, I can't imagine what a kid is supposed to do with that. And, as a kid myself, I didn't know what to do with it. I didn't, I tell you, I don't even know if I knew it was true. But what I did know from my own personality is when someone is sad you always try to give them hope. That's what I had been trained to do. That's what I learned to do. So, even at that moment, that wasn't about me, you know. And then my mother's death was the first funeral I had attended (cries).

Q: Who told you she had died?

A: Oh, so I came home from my first day of high school. My father was such a goof. On the rotary dial phone, he had two teenage kids living in the house, so he had a lock on the phone, because we were always on the phone and there was no call waiting in those days. And across the street from us was a drug store with a pay phone. So it was very common for either Jane or me to be across the street on the phone. You could talk as long as you wanted to for that dime too. So I had come home from school, and I was in the phone booth. And my sister's friend, Jeanie, came and knocked on the door of the phone booth and said, "You need to come home." It was late afternoon. It wasn't dark out. It was fall. I mean, it was September the fourth. I remember it still being day, but it could have been five o'clock at night, but I don't remember. And I came into the house. I can't remember who told me, but it's one of those things where you walk into someplace and you know.

I'm going to talk about Maggie again now, simply because she was in kindergarten. And there was some talk about whether she goes to the funeral or doesn't go to the funeral. It was decided that she wasn't going to go to the funeral. And she was in a kindergarten program at the preschool that she had gone to because it was an all-day program. With my mom being sick, I think that that's what the family had decided. So at the day of my mother's funeral, Maggie went to school. She was dressed and sent to school. I don't know what people told her. I honest-to-God don't. And I know that's not my story, but it is my story, when I think of how sad that must have been for her.

And so, my father came from the Orthodox tradition. We weren't raised Orthodox, but it was sitting shivah on fruit crates and covering the mirrors and the whole spiel. And I had never been to a funeral. Now, I have this crazy recollection, and nobody else in my family has it, so it's probably not true. I remember this open casket, which does not fit with any of this Orthodox stuff at all. Somehow I remember this with my mother, and I remember it being in public. Because I remember what she was wearing. I don't know how in touch we are with our emotions at such a time of huge loss.

When the family came back to our apartment, and there were lots of people and lots of food and lots of talk and some laughter and some conversation, but I thought it was horrible. And my friends came, and I remember how they walked into the door with the look of fear on their faces. You know, it was like they were thinking, "It could be my mom," and "Who are you now and what does it mean?" And my response was, "I don't want you to feel uncomfortable, so I'm going to let you know that I'm OK," sitting with my friends in my bedroom. But I know, at one point, Rhoda told me, actually, that she remembers going into the bedroom and just sitting and talking. But I was feeling some real anger and confusion, and remember just going into the bedroom and crying. And you had asked me did I tell anybody about it, and I didn't. I didn't.

And, you know, the whole thing about this experience and talking about this is good, and Jane and I have begun to do some talking. It's comfortable to talk to my sisters about this now. It is. But we all remember it just a little bit differently. And I remember telling you that I don't know how little Maggie . . . I don't know who told her, what they told her, how they told her. I don't. . . .

Q: Do you remember Maggie at the shivah?

A: I'm not going to say I remember Maggie at the shivah, but I know she was there. That was one of those times where I don't remember looking after her or trying to.

Q: Maybe she was put to bed.

A: I don't think . . . I think it's probably pretty hard in a shivah house. It wasn't a big place. People were in the kitchen, they were in the dining room, they were in the living room, friends were in my bedroom with me.

Q: Tell us about the first day back at school.

A: When I went back to school, and this was my first year at the big high school, Mather High School. And the attendance office required that, when you came back after an absence, that you had to bring a note. And I know my note said "Please excuse Julia's absence. Her mother has died, and we were sitting shivah." A simple note like that. But the woman that I spoke to when I got to school—and I didn't know anybody at this high school—looked at me and said, "You were out seven days!" in a stern voice. And I remember, it's funny, when I think about it now. My father didn't bring me to school that day. Or if he did, he dropped me off. I was only a kid. I was only 14 years old. But it was kind of my responsibility. And this woman was very insensitive. And I remember looking back at her and directly saying to her, "My mother died." And it didn't make a difference. It didn't make a difference, like "Oh my God, I'm so sorry," or "Oh." It [was] just, "Here's your pass, go to class. "

Q: Did you visit her grave after her funeral?

A: My dad missed my mother terribly and wanted to go to the cemetery on some kind of regular basis. But after he married Katrina [Kat], it was difficult. So I would go to the cemetery with my dad, and it was, kind of, like we couldn't tell Kat. We weren't allowed to tell. We would always make up some story we were going to do something else.

So, sometimes, Maggie and I would go to the cemetery without my dad. I don't know why. I don't know why. I think it was just too messy for all three of us to go under this secret. So I think Maggie and I went. I think it was OK with Kat if we went on Mother's Day. It's crazy. I'm from that generation where nobody knew what the hell they were doing. I don't think anybody meant any harm, although she, Kat, certainly could have been more generous with her attitude being a parent herself. Maggie and Kat never got along very well, and I'm not quite sure why. But they didn't.

Anyway, I remember taking Maggie to the cemetery. My mom is buried at Westlawn. And standing there with her and putting my arms around her, and I was sad and I was crying, and here I was with this little girl (tearful). And Maggie was a teenager before we really talked much, and she said, "I don't remember anything."

Q: Your mom died in September. Your birthday is in December. Do you have any memories of that first birthday after she died?

A: You know, I don't remember the birthday. What I remember is President Kennedy died. I remember that. I remember President Kennedy died on November twenty-second. My father's birthday is December the sixth, and mine is December the seventh. I was 15. I was turning 15.

Q: What do you remember about his death, Kennedy's death?

A: I just remember my father coming home and walking in the door and looking broken, looking like he couldn't hold his shoulders up. And then when he walked through the door, he just broke down and started to cry. I think the grief—I was thinking about this as I was driving over here—my father loved my mother so much, and I don't think he ever got over it. I don't think people ever get over this period. I think that's what I am beginning to learn. But my father truly didn't. And he came through the door, and he started to cry. And I grew up seeing my father cry. Some people don't. That was a comfort. Ironically, it didn't allow me to cry. Maybe it wasn't a comfort. Maybe seeing him cry just allowed that part of me to comfort him.

And what I've grown to learn, but only recently, not 10 years ago and certainly not 20 or 30 years ago, is how important it is to let it out and to talk about it.

When you ask me about my birthday, when I think about that thought, it just is gray to me. It's not necessarily gray and cold, but it's gray. It's like one long period without specific days. And if you ask me when the light came back in, I'm not sure I could tell you. I need to think. My birthday's in December, and I don't even remember moving. This was the apartment that we had lived in when my mother was alive. Soon after she died we had sold some furniture, and then we moved into this building, brand-new building.

Q: Do you remember the Jewish holiday? The Jewish New Year very soon after your mother died?

A: I don't remember the Jewish holidays. I remember taking a trip to California during winter break and visiting my father's family. Those are the pictures where we all have these fancy-schmantzy coats and boots and all this stuff. That whole time felt very surreal. I didn't know how to either express my needs or know that it was OK to let somebody know I even had needs. So that's a double whammy.

Q: Julia, what about that first Thanksgiving? Do you remember that as well?

A: We probably spent it with Rhoda's family. Rhoda's mother did not particularly, she didn't dislike my father, but she didn't have a lot of patience for his impatience. But she really reached . . . she treated me like a daughter, and so did my uncle, my Uncle Alex. Except they lived on the west side. They lived in Austin. OK? And we were in Rogers Park. So that was a considerable distance, you know. My father also had a cousin who was older than he who lived in Rogers Park, and sometimes we'd spend holidays with them. But that was kind of like going to somebody's house where you were invited but you didn't really know the people as opposed. . . .

Q: You were 15 at that first birthday, so the Jewish holidays would have come, and you would have gone to your first Yizkor service [memorial service].

A: Yeah, I do remember that. Actually, that was really spooky, because my mother died September fourth, and the Jewish holiday is always the following week.

My father went to Yizkor services every single morning. That was the way he grew up. I'm a reformed Jew now, and in my congregation when it's time to say Kaddish [mourner's prayer], everyone stands up. But, in those days, and I didn't know anything about this, I went to a service across the street from my house in the park-district building. And so, there was this teenage service, and I remember going. And to this day, I still don't know if I have it right, I don't know if you do stand up the first year, if you don't stand up the first year. I did. I don't remember if my sister Jane was with me, but if you think about the dynamic of that, this was not a room with adults who have lost their adult parents. This is a room of kids, teenagers. So I remember standing, and I do remember this— I remember thinking, "I'm supposed to stand," but it didn't feel right, it didn't feel wrong. It was like I knew I was going to stand up, and there were going to be very few other people standing up. And I do remember that moment. And then it happened again the following week for Yom Kippur.

I have this real issue about people who experience a loss. I'm a really good friend and very devoted to people while they're going through this experience and someone is sick. And if someone tells me that their father died, even if I don't know the person well, or their mother died, it just brings such grief to my heart. So I don't remember Thanksgiving that year. I do remember the Jewish holidays. I can't tell you where we spent them.

Oh, you know what, you know what, I do remember. My father had an aunt; her name was Francis. And Francis was a great cook, and she made fabulous sweet-and-sour meatballs. She was a pain in the ass, but she was, she was really a good cook. And she loved my father, and we went there.

And then, for winter break, which was December, my mother passed away in September, we went to California. That was an unusual experience, because here you are with all this family. Now this is family that I grew up with, because I was born in California, and I really hadn't lived in Chicago that many years before my mother died. So this was family that I knew pretty well. And I think I carried some resentment. I would have loved it if one of my aunts would have taken me out to lunch and said, "How are you doing?" and "I miss your mom. I bet you miss your mom," or whatever. I don't know what the script needed to be, but everything was done in this damn unit. I mean, that's how we did it in my family. Sixteen people got in cars, and we all went to the same place. And the whole idea that people might have needed some separateness or had different relationships with people didn't exist.

My father just loved Mildred, his brother's wife, and Mildred was like the earth mother, and she's still alive today. When my father died she would call me because she missed him. And she would say, "How are you doing?" And she knew my father's birthday, she knew forever and ever, and she knew my birthday was the next day. And she would call me from California, and we would talk. But no one did that after my mother died.

If I were a father who had young kids and my wife had died, I think, in addition to talking about it in my own home, I would get those women friends and aunts and uncles who had always been part of the family, not just to continue to do family things, but somehow give a child a chance to talk on an individual basis, not in a big setting. Now my Aunt Francis would do this with me and Rhoda.

Although, when I got older, my Aunt Francis and I would go and have lunch sometimes. If I asked her about my mother, it was always this saintly . . . but there was never anything at all about, "Oh, God, your mom used to get so mad at this," or "I can make her laugh by this," or "She loved Frank Sinatra," or anything. It was always "She was so patient and so sweet, and everyone loved Julia, and you're just like Julia." This being just like Julia is a blessing and a curse. But I would much prefer that than what my father said about Maggie. "She's so cute, but! . . . " It was kind of like the joke in the family. And then Jane, poor Jane was the rebel without a clue. And I think she did have a clue. I mean, all she wanted to say is "Love me. Love me as I am. I'm doing the best I can." But nobody knew how to say any of those things in those days.

But the interesting thing about my father . . . he was very proud of me as a person. I mean, he, my father, could say to me, "You are really a person of value. I really like who you are." And sometimes kids never have those conversations. And I don't think my father articulated that with too many other people. But he used to say I was the only one who really loved him. There was some kind of acceptance that my father yearned for that somehow he felt with me.

Q: Tell us about the memories you have of your mother.

A: You know, I wish someday I could unlock more. But I picture my mother . . . well, actually there's a lot of things. But they're mostly in the house. But the story that I think of is my mother washing dishes at the sink and singing. And singing "Summertime" from Porgy and Bess. And singing "My Yiddisha Mama," which she taught me and I sang with her. But I think I also used to sing with my father too. I remember singing at the kitchen sink with my mother (cries).

Q: Julia, tell us about the stone setting.

A: My mother was buried at Westlawn Cemetery. The stories about visiting my mom's grave with Maggie and having to do that in secret are pretty powerful. You know, again, I never learned, I don't know if there's a right way, how to go to a cemetery or what you say or what you do. I don't think people know. But last time I was there, which was really last summer, it was the last day of school, and I said I'm going to go to my mother's grave. I'm going to go to my father's grave. I'm going to talk to both of them. I don't know what the hell I'm going to say, but I'm going to go. And I did. And I stood there and I talked and I cried (cries).

My mother's stone setting, God, it had to have been so hard for my dad, because look how young they were. Who had a funeral? Who had a gravesite? Who owned a gravesite? My father had no money. I think I told you he had changed professions and moved to Chicago and was working two jobs. I think I told you that he was working at the post office at night. My mom was working for an insurance company at night. It was hard. It was really hard for them.

Q: Do you remember the stone setting?

A: Not really.

Q: That's what I thought. All right. Tell us about how your father told you about Kat and getting remarried.

A: Well it was kind of a non-issue for me. It was, I think I might have been amused that my father was dating. I never felt threatened by it. Never. I think that's a genuine response. I think a lot of it had to do with my comfort level in how much my father had loved my mother. And I knew that. I knew that. . . . Kat and my father and Jane and Maggie and I went to dinner at Augustino's downtown on Rush Street on a Saturday night, and that's how we met Kat.

Q: Did you know you were going to meet her?

A: Yes. My father actually wasn't much of a talker about those kinds of things. So I think, and this is one of those memories where you don't know if it's real or you just manufactured it or someone told it to you so many times, but I think my dad said something like, and I think he needed to say it this way, "I've been really lonely, and there's somebody who I think I'd like to spend some time with." And then later on that same kind of response, " . . . and I think we're going to get married."

Q: How did you feel when you met her?

A: It was fine. Do I remember Jane and I talking about it? No. You would think we would have. Anyway . . . the wedding was on a Wednesday. Who the hell gets married on a Wednesday? My father doesn't have to see patients on Wednesday, so you have to get married on a Wednesday! It made perfect sense to me, but I knew it was insane. It wasn't a big wedding, but Alex and Francis and Kat had a sister and a brother. So everybody had to take the day off on Wednesday so Alfred could get married!

Q: What do you remember?

A: What do I remember? Actually, I went shopping with Kat for the suit that she wore. She invited me to do that with her. And that seemed OK, too. Is that weird? Is that weird that I didn't mind that stuff? I don't think I mind it. I actually liked her well enough, OK? So the wedding was, it wasn't in a rabbi's study, but it was in a temple, not in a sanctuary, a room in a temple, and I want to say 11:00 A.M. or 1:00 P.M., and they got married, and then everybody went out to lunch. Kat was only 29 years old, and she thought that she was going to bake my father sunshine cakes and live happily ever after. Well, it wasn't true then, it ain't true now, and it will never be true. So she really bit off a huge thing. She pretty much left me alone.

Q: How old were you?

A: I had turned 16 in December, and they got married March 10. And there was some question about should I or should I not invite her to my Sweet Sixteen, and I chose not to. OK? I think I just said I'd be more comfortable. I don't know how to talk to people about this. And so I didn't.

Q: Who was with you for your Sweet Sixteen?

A: My father and a neighbor.

Q: What was that like, a Sweet Sixteen without your mother?

A: I think I was in the dead zone. You know, when you ask me these questions, I mean I did everything, and everybody around me seemed relatively pleased that we were doing all the right things. So you do the right things, but you don't really, you don't live in the moment. Honestly, you really don't live in the moment. You should get up on the morning of your Sweet Sixteen and bawl your damn eyes out saying, "Shit, I'm 16 years old, and my mother's not here." You should. And I'm not a big person for shoulds, but there ought to be a comfort level in your house where you can do that. You can go up to somebody in your house and say, "I feel sad today. I know this is a happy occasion, but OK?" So when you say that I've been carrying all this stuff for 40 years, I'll probably come some Monday and tell you about my Sweet Sixteen, but right now it's kind of like we did it, and it was pleasant, and my friends all came, and my mother's friends came, and some of my girl-friends' mothers came.

Q: And your graduation?

A: My graduation from high school? My father was married to Kat already. They got married when I was 16. I graduated high school. Actually, I was 17. They had been married about a year and a half. And it was, by that time, it was like every-body else. Do you remember there was a place on Ridge and Clark called Towne and Country? OK. So in those days, you went to a graduation, and everyone went out there for ice cream or a sandwich. So I did what everybody else did. That was the thing.

Q: What about when you got married?

A: The story about when I got married was really about my Aunt Esther who looked so much like my mother. The truth . . . I'll tell you. I think planning a wedding is difficult for people, and nobody expects good things to be stressful. And I was no spring chicken. I wasn't 19 or 20. I was 28 years old, and I had already lived out of the house, and I had been teaching for several years. And it wasn't as though this was difficult. Frank's dad was pretty amenable to things. My father was really happy. I was always glad to be able to make my father happy. And I'm very aware of that. So my sister who ran off and got married in a Catholic church—at least this daughter is going to get married by a rabbi. She's marrying someone who's not Jewish, but they're going to get married by a rabbi, and my father can walk me down an aisle. And actually that was pretty cool. That was very cool. But my Aunt Esther, who is my mother's youngest sister, 9 years younger than she, came to the wedding. And I had not seen her for a long time. I can't tell you how many years it was, but it was a long time. And she looks so much like my mother that the first time I saw her that weekend was at the wedding. Why didn't I see her the night before? You know, there was all this crap in my family. Kat was very uncomfortable with my mother's family. But there was a prenuptial dinner. And I'm trying to think why the heck my mother's family wasn't there, but they weren't. That's really terrible.

Q: Maybe Kat didn't permit them.

A: I mean, I can't remember the details on that, but I do know on the day I got married I did not see Esther until I walked down the aisle. And it struck me, it was like having my mother sit there. She had an aisle seat, and it was right near the front. And I looked up, and she looked up at me, and it just . . . my father fell apart, we all fell apart. And Esther will tell that story. My mother and her sisters were very close. And I should really spend more time with Esther. Esther might be the one to tell me some good stories.

Q: Tell us about the telling of family stories, the Alfred stories that you tell on his birthday.

A: Oh, the stories that I share with Allen?

Q: And why is that important, the telling of stories?

A: I think the telling of stories are important because that's what you have, you have memories and memories don't ever have to die. And memories are a way of understanding who you are, and where you got to be who you are, and why you have these wonderful traits, and why you have some schtick, and why you have a sense of humor, and just where it comes from. I believe that so, so strongly. So when Allen [son] was little and probably three or four or five, my birthday has always been the day after my dad's, and I guess I got the idea once that we would start to tell Alfred stories. And so I would take the box of pictures and tell him stories about Alfred and us.

Q: Did you ever tell Allen your mother stories?

A: You know, Allen knows that I struggle with this. But I do tell him some stories. My mother would tell me she wanted to go on a diet and would I help her. And I tell him about singing at the sink with my mother. I knew my mother struggled. I always stood back and watched that my sister was hard, and my mother was trying her best to really look after Jane and help Jane get through this. And then when Maggie was born, it was wonderful. It was a wonderful to have this baby in the house. And my mother taught me so much about mothering and singing and loving.

Q: Which brings me to my next question: What was the birth of Allen like without your mother?

A: I've talked to so many people about this, and I bet you guys have in your practice too, when you meet women who are pregnant or have a child and their mother is gone. It's huge. I think you go through your whole life having this hole in your heart, but you don't know, you don't know, it's so contradictory. You know, here's this joy, this beautiful child, and thank God, a healthy, beautiful child, and you're so happy, and at the same moment there's this longing. Kat was there, and Kat did her best to love my kid, but it's not the same thing. And it's funny, I'm really lucky in this regard. I told you my Aunt Francis, Rhoda's mother, always treated Allen like he was a grandson. And I can't thank her enough (tears). She passed away years ago. I can't thank her or my uncle enough for doing that because you want someone to love your child. You want your child . . . your child is always special to you (tears).

Maybe this is a romantic view. I imagine some people have some nasty grandparents. But generally speaking, grandparents kvell from their grandchildren, and my father wasn't there, and my mother wasn't there. Frank's dad was wonderful. Frank's dad really did love Allen. Coming home from the hospital with a brand new baby is hard, and Kat came over the first night, and she cut Allen's nails, and she helped me bathe him and probably did the things that mothers do when their children become mothers as well. But I was very, very aware of this big loss, and questions I wanted to ask, and I think there was envy, not from a mean point of view, but, I mean, I think that's when I really started to kind of suffer over this. I went into a restaurant—I told you this—and here's a mother or people who look like mother and daughter having lunch together, and I just envy it, not meanly, I just envy it. And I'm not intolerant or impatient, but I do think there's an edge to me when people start to complain about their mothers. You know now, people our age have parents who are ill and that's different. But you know like 10 and 20 years ago, when their mothers were too controlling or their mothers were too this or that. . . . And I found myself saying, "I bet it really is hard for you, but I really wish I had a mother." And this morning I was just thinking I wish had someone to take care of me. I just want someone to love me who doesn't go away (cries hard).

Q: But you also had a hard time when you turned 39 which was the age your mother was when she died.

A: Right. My marriage was falling apart when I was 39. Allen was little, and Allen and I had a really good solid relationship all the way through. What I was aware of at that time is I've always been surrounded by a lot of people who love me, and people who not only love me but cared for me and cared about me. But it's not the same thing as having a mother who says, "I'll come over" or "Bring him over here, let him stay here for the night," or "You need some time." Now that's a romantic view. I don't know who has that kind of mother, but that's what I think.

And it's funny. I wrote a poem about who I am and what my hopes are, and the final lines in the poem are about I hope to be a grandmother who spoils my grandchildren and greets them with hugs and kisses, and is greeted with hugs and kisses, and let's them stay up too late and tells them stories. I mean that's what I wanted. That's what I would love to be able to do. And I think it's for myself. It has to do with Allen not having *my* mom.

Q: The do's and don'ts, if you were giving advice to a parent?

A: I think you need to talk. You don't want to be overbearing, but I think you err on the side of saying too much than saying too little. I think rituals are really important, and I think rituals can be established in very nonthreatening ways. They don't have to be at the anniversary of someone's death. It's a parent who has the sense to say this kid needs some time alone with me. If there's two or three siblings in the house say, "We're going to do our own bedtime story," or "Mom used to like to read you this book." Suggest bringing those memories in or playing the music or singing the songs. You know my Alfred thing, maybe celebrating the anniversary of a person's birthday, not necessarily their death. I don't do anything with my kid about the anniversary of the death. I will say to him, "This is the date my mother died," and I'll light a Yahzreit candle, but that's not the same thing as celebrating the birthday.

I think the thing I said to you earlier, asking those adults and people in your life who know your child to stay in touch to encourage them and to be honest enough to say your kid needs this and you probably do too. I think the adults need to acknowledge what he or she needs, and if they're in touch with that, they're probably more able to provide it for their kid. But if they're in denial about their own needs, how the hell do they know what somebody else might want? But we have a generation of people that are so incredibly needy, they think the whole world should stop because they have suffered a moment of grief. And then we have people who bury it. So there has to be something in between.

So what else can you teach kids? Well, even before someone dies, you teach them it's OK to ask. They're not always going to hear the answer that they want, but teach them it's OK to ask. I was never taught it's OK to ask, it's OK to say no, it's OK. If you're a compliant kid, you make it work even if you jump through hoops.

Q: You talked about giving the child permission to be sad.

A: That starts before someone passes away in the family. If you've been allowed to feel sad and be able to go up to somebody and say, "Oh I'm so sad today. I lost my bike or my best friend was mean to me," and have someone acknowledge that. . . . I think parents say, "Oh I'm sorry. Is there something I can do to help?" I swear to God, if people could just learn those words—*is there something I can do to help* and *how are you.* Most of us, children as well as adults, probably won't ask for anything other than just let me talk to you, just listen. And ask them not in just a cursory way.

Q: You didn't have much interaction with your mom's sisters? Why was that?

A: I think there's probably two or three or four reasons. It would have been helpful. I didn't because in my father's new marriage it was not encouraged to continue that relationship. But honestly, my mother's sisters were not really crazy about my father. They thought my father did not make an easy life for my mother because of his anger sometimes. I told you, I think it was 20 before I went back to California after that winter trip just after my mother died. So I went to California for the first time and got a lot of questions from people "Why have you not been?" And I said, "You know, I think—I remember saying it—it's just too hard." And I really had never gone back there looking for memories of my mother. I probably should. I probably should go back.

Q: You said there were four reasons.

A: One of them was I was discouraged by Kat. One of them was my own way of just not wanting to let it in. One of them was they didn't make the effort. I think they felt unwelcome. I'm not saying that in any kind of a negative thing toward them. And I think I didn't know that it would be OK to contact them. And I know now that it would have been. It would have been absolutely OK, and it probably would have been better than OK if I had said to my dad, "I want to stay in touch with Esther and Sylvia," because he loved the fact that I stayed in touch with Francis and Alex, even though he didn't himself because Kat didn't feel comfortable with that. And Francis, my mother's best friend, really did make an effort to try to keep some kind of a social thing going there.

Q: After your mom died initially, around 14, 15, did you have bad dreams? Did you have sicknesses? And who took care of you if you did?

A: I don't remember my dreams often. However, this summer, I was with my sister Jane—and this is so weird. She's my love sister, and I've always loved her. And she has not always made it easy. But she's just always loved me so much, and there was never a doubt in my mind, even when she was screaming and yelling at me. But this summer, I was sharing something with her about Allen, and she hugged me to say good-bye. And I remember feeling that my mother was hugging me. I mean, it was like this out-of-body kind of spiritual experience. And I didn't tell her. I just remember driving home in the car still having that tingly sense. Isn't that weird, that this had happened? And it's not the kind of thing you go telling people, because they think you're whacked. But you know, it was just something about that hug that really touched my heart. It was like my mother was giving me that hug. I forgot what your question was.

Oh, dreams. And I think that's dreaming in another sense. It's like a wish. It's a wish kind of a dream. I have a lot of those.

Q: And when you were sick, because you must have had colds or flus, after she died, who took care of you?

A: You know, I don't remember being sick in high school. I think I was the kind of kid who didn't want to stay home sick.

Q: After your mother died, was there anything of hers that you wanted that you got?

A: I didn't think I wanted anything. It's not that I didn't want things, I just wasn't aware of wanting things. When I get dressed I always put on something that I got myself. Always. But I don't have my mother's ring. My sister took my mother's wedding ring. My father gave my sister my mother's jewelry, and they didn't have a lot of money, so it really wasn't much. But they took all the wedding bands and took all the diamonds and made other kinds of jewelry. There were these hurricane lamps that I really did not care for. My father thought they were really important to hang on to. So they were in the house all the way through Kat's life. And they were offered to me. My sister has them now. I didn't want them. It's not like I don't want them, I just didn't want them. I had my mother's china. But I honestly wish I had had something simple, like a bathrobe, a simple . . . even if it were costume jewelry, I would wear it. What I do have—oh, I forgot about this—I should have brought it. My father gave my mother a pin when they were dating, and she loved it. And it's jade, it's a fish and in the middle of the fish is a watch. The watch never ran. I have that.

Q: What did they do with all your mother's things?

A: You know, I don't even know who came and did that, you know, packed them up and gave them to the ARK or whatever. I don't know. I have a pair of my father's bedroom slippers that I just keep hanging; I keep them in the closet.

I do have my mother's watch. I have some things of my grandmother's. I have my mother's china. I think I told you, Jane had the china, and she broke a whole bunch of it. You know what I do have? My mother had a set of silverplate silverware in a wooden box, like everybody has. And Kat used it for years in addition to whatever she had, because you know, for fancy stuff, you never have enough. And Louise, Kat's daughter, last summer brought them to me and said, "You know this is your mother's, and you probably want it." I don't have the box, but I do have all the silverware. So I have that. The watch is kind of special. But I wish it were an old flannel shirt or a pillowcase or something.

When my father died, I remember going to his office the next day like I had to go and get something. And my father always changed clothes when he went to work. So, on the back of his office door was a pair of pants and the gown that he wore. And I just remember standing there smelling it. A smell doesn't last forever, but something that someone wore, I think, is really powerful. Do I think a little girl or a little boy should have something like that? Yeah. Do I think that it should be in their room? Not in a spooky way. I think it's how you do things, how you do things. If Maggie were this big, and she were wearing my mother's bathrobe and walking through the house with it trailing behind her, it would have been wonderful, just to have it.

Q: We have a little girl's story, in the book, whose mother died when she was about Maggie's age. She was actually a little younger. And her father let her choose one of the mother's sweatshirts, and she slept in it, and it came down to the floor. And then later, he took a couple of shirts and gave them to the son and the daughter to choose one of the shirts of the mother's, and he had teddy bears made out of them. Isn't that a lovely thing to do? Because it's something to hold on to, and initially, to smell that scent.

A: Yeah, it's for real. You just have to see the value in it though. And I don't know how you teach people the value of that, because I think they're so afraid of the pain. I guess one thing I want to say to honor both of my parents is, "This is painful, but I have this desire to talk about it." I must have gotten that from them. I mean, I had 14 years of my mother. And while she wasn't a talker, and she did not reveal what was painful, and I was not encouraged in those days. Something about both of those people taught me that there is a value in doing it.

Q: What name would you like us to call you in the book?

A: Julia. My mother's name.

Maggie

Q: Tell us about the memories you have of your mother being sick.

A: I don't have any memories of my mother being sick. In fact, I don't have any memories at all of her. I was five years old. I probably was about three when she first got sick, and I don't have any memories of that time, of her being sick. I was never taken to the hospital. I don't remember her being in the hospital. I don't remember anything. In fact, I have no memories of that time at all. None at all.

Q: Do you have any early memories?

A: No. No. I don't remember anything. I have no memories.

Q: Well then, tell us about your earliest memory? What is the earliest thing you can remember?

A: Oh, that's funny. I do remember something. Gee, and my mom was in that memory. My dad had bought this new dining room set, and he was very proud about it. And I remember I put cherry tomatoes in a bowl on the dinning room table, and my father, who had a terrible temper, started screaming at me, and my mother got me away.

Q: Oh, so she protected you?

A: Yeah, I guess you could say she protected me. She got me out of that and took the bowl away. So I guess I do have a memory, you could say, of my mother, because I do remember that. And how angry my dad was and how scared I was.

Q: Do you have any memories of who told you that your mother had died?

A: No. Nobody told me. I don't remember anything. I don't remember who told me. Someone must have told me, but I don't remember who. I don't know how I found out. I don't even remember finding out. I've been told that I went to nursery school. I had been in kindergarten, but when my mom got sick, they put me back into nursery school because it was a full-day program so I could be cared for, because my mother was sick and couldn't take care of me during the day. . . . And I know, I was told that I went to nursery school on the day of the funeral.

The day my mother died, it must have been like the first day of kindergarten, maybe it was the second, I don't remember. But I've been told that they took me out of kindergarten and put me back into nursery school because I knew all the people in nursery school, and so they felt that was best for me. And I was also told that I didn't go to the funeral, that I just went to nursery school. So I didn't remember that. I don't even remember them going to the funeral. I have no memories of that time. I was also told that the nursery-school people were very nice to me, and they kept me all day, and then they took me out to dinner that night. But I don't really remember that, and I don't remember coming home.

Q: Do you remember people being sad when you came home or in the next few days? There must have been the Jewish shivah.

A: No, I don't remember that at all. I have no memories at all.

Q: Do you remember anything after your mother died, like the Jewish holidays, Thanksgiving, Christmas?

A: No. I have no memories, none at all.

Q: Tell us about your dad meeting Kat or marrying Kat. What do you remember about that?

A: Oh, *that* I remember! We were all taken out to dinner, and I spent the night at her house. Kat had two children. I was about six and Louise, her daughter was seven, and Tom, her son, was eight. So we went out to dinner, and I remember that I spent the night at her house, and I was really excited. It was a sleepover. It was so exciting. Tom and Louise were there and I don't remember anything other than being excited. I was pleased to be there.

Q: What do you remember after your dad married Kat?

A: Oh, I've got a funny memory of that. I remember going to sleep and waking up the next morning, and I was really excited because I had a mommy. And they must have come back from their honeymoon, and I was so excited to have a mommy. And I remember running into the kitchen with a big smile on my face and saying, "Hello, Mommy." And Louise and Tom were standing there with her, and they all laughed. And I remember thinking I will never call her Mommy again, and I never did. I called her Kat from that day onwards, and I never called her anything else. And my father, who I adored, would beg me to call her Mommy, because she wanted me to call her Mommy, or maybe he wanted me to call her Mommy, and I wouldn't. And I knew that that would please him, and I would do anything to please my dad, but I wouldn't do it—I wouldn't call her Mommy.

Q: Growing up with Kat and her two children, did you have to share a room, or did you have your own room?

A: No. Louise and I shared a room, and Louise and I are great friends. I've always loved Louise, and we are so close. We speak about three times a week, even now, and we're just very, very close. Tom I never really got on with, and I don't care that much about him. I've always just thought of Louise as my sister. We're terribly close. In fact, recently, Jane, my older sister, wanted to take me out for my birthday for lunch, and she said to me it will be the three Silverman girls; Jane, Julia, and me. And I said, "Oh, are Louise and Pam invited, because I think of them as my sisters too?" Pam is my stepbrother Tom's wife. They weren't invited, because I think Jane really

doesn't have much to do with them at all. She hated Kat. I
didn't like Kat really, myself. I mean, it's not like I was badly
treated by her. I was always fed and well clothed, but she
never gave me anything really more than that. She wasn't
warm to me, and I didn't really feel loved by her.

Q: Did she treat you differently to her own children? Maybe she
was threatened by you?

A: She could have been jealous of me because my father loved me
so much. I was this cute little girl, and I'd lost my mother, and
he just, I was his favorite. He just loved me. She was never
very warm to me. In fact, there were a couple of things that
happened when I was growing up. My cousin, Donny, was
getting married in California, and he asked me to be a bridesmaid.

Q: How come he asked you to be a bridesmaid? Did you know
him well?

A: Well, I had gone out to California in the summer, and I had
gone camping with Donny and his fiancée and the whole
family. And we had a wonderful time. It was just a great summer. And we were all in the camp together, and that's when I
really got to know him. So when he was getting married, he
asked me to be a bridesmaid, and I was not allowed to be a
bridesmaid, because Louise wasn't asked to be a bridesmaid.
She wasn't asked. And I was terribly upset about it, but I was
not allowed to be a bridesmaid. Kat felt that everything had to
be the same.

Q: So you weren't a bridesmaid?

A: No. I wasn't a bridesmaid. I remember that my dad and Kat
went to the wedding, but I didn't. Louise wasn't a bridesmaid,
so I wasn't going to be a bridesmaid. If Louise had been
invited to be a bridesmaid, that would have made it OK. In
fact, it was the same thing with our weddings. We were getting married around the same time, within six months of each
other. And this neighbor of ours who had been wonderful to
me, and, in fact, I remained close with her always. Her name
was Sandy. She was just wonderful to me after my mother
died, and I was taken into that family. I would go there for dinner and sleep over after my mother died, and they were just
very, very good to me. So when I was getting married, Sandy,

the mother, took me to look for a dress. And we found one. But Kat made me go with *her* to look for a dress. So she took me shopping. And we had to have identical weddings: same place, same time of day, everything had to be absolutely the same.

Q: Did you like the dress that Sandy had chosen? Would you rather have had that dress?

A: No. It was OK. The dress I got with Kat was fine. Our weddings had to be the same. Louise and I had to have exactly the same sort of wedding. I married into this very wealthy German-Jewish family, and they would have wanted a much fancier wedding on a Saturday night at the Drake Hotel. But I had to get married on a Sunday, just like Louise, and have the same exact wedding. I said to my in-laws at the time, "My father can't afford the sort of wedding that you want me to have," and I was not going to do that to my dad. Although he would have done anything for me, but I wasn't going to make him pay for the sort of wedding that they would have wanted.

Q: It sounds like Kat wasn't very compassionate with you.

A: Well, I do have a memory of my parents-in-law asking Kat to come to Thanksgiving dinner after my dad died. And it was very kind of them to include her, but she refused because Louise and Tom weren't invited.

Q: What was Kat like when you had your first child?

A: You know, I had a miscarriage, and I remember Alfred coming to the hospital and just crying and crying over me. I wasn't that upset, because I just had gotten married. But he cried and cried over me. With my first child, Kat bought the layette, and she kept that at her house for me. But I didn't want anyone at the hospital with me, so nobody came. She never babysat for my children, but she babysat for Louise and Tom's children all the time. She never offered to babysit for my children. And at their first birthday party, she called the day of the party and said she wasn't coming. I've never forgotten that.

    You know, I took care of Kat when she got ill. I went there almost every day and really took care of her.

Q: How did you feel when Kat died?

A: It was OK.

Q: Maggie, how did you decide to become a nurse, or why did you decide to become a nurse?

A: I don't know. I've always wanted to be a nurse from when I was very, very little. I always wanted to be a nurse.

Q: How old? What is very, very little?

A: Oh, I don't know, five, six, seven.

Q: Maggie, that was the time, five, six, seven, when your mom had died. Do you think it could have been after your mother died that you decided that you wanted to be a nurse?

A: I don't know. I just knew that I always wanted to be a nurse since I was very, very little.

Q: Perhaps, Maggie, you wanted to be a nurse because you wanted to take care of people in the way that you would have liked to have been taken care of by a loving woman like a mother, or perhaps you wanted to take care of people like you would have wanted your mom to be taken care of? And, in that way, you were trying to make people better, because you had wanted someone to make your mom better?

A: I don't know.

Q: Well, what kind of a nurse were you? Did you specialize in anything?

A: I used to work in intensive care.

Q: We remember from Jane and Julia that your mom was in intensive care for quite a while. Do you think there could have been a link there?

A: I don't know. Maybe.

Q: Do you have any other memories of growing up? What about when you were a child? Any memories growing up of your mom?

A: I do remember my dad late at night crying and crying, carrying a picture of my mom, and sobbing and crying. I remember that.

Q: Do you remember ever going to the cemetery perhaps to see your mom's grave or going to the graveyard on the anniversary of her death?

A: Yeah, yeah. I would go to the grave with Julia. She would take me, and she would cry and cry, and I would stand there and say a prayer. I would chant it over and over again, the prayers.

Q: Who taught you the prayer?

A: I don't know. I just knew it. And I would chant it over and over again.

Q: Do you have anything of your mother's?

A: Yeah, I have a photograph of her that I put on the mantelpiece. She looks just like Julia. In fact, my kids, when they first saw the photo, looked up and said, "That's Julia." I have a photo of her. I also have something that Jane gave me. Jane must have had my mother's wedding ring or something and rearranged or took out the diamonds and made up other stuff, and I have something from that.

You know, Kat lived for many years after my father died. My father was a lot older than Kat. She was only 29 when she married my father, and I think he was like 41, 42, 43, something like that. So she lived many years after him. He died when he was 59. After Kat died, Tom, my brother, my step-brother, sold the house. But I never saw anything from that. There was no money or anything. And I never asked Tom. Maybe Tom used the money to pay medical bills for Kat. I don't know. We never got anything, but I didn't care even though. . . . Whatever there was, Louise and Tom got it all. There was nothing that I knew about.

Q: Do you go to your dad's grave? And where is Kat buried?

A: Kat is buried next to my dad. My mom is buried in a different cemetery. She is buried in Westlawn. I know a lot of people where the first wife is buried next to the husband and then the second wife is there too. But Kat would never have that. So it's just the two of them are buried there. In fact, I went to a family funeral a while ago. It was kind of crazy. On the day of the funeral, someone else from the family also died. And I went to see my dad's grave before the funeral. And as I got close to it I saw that Tom and Louise were there, and so I walked away, because I knew I would be coming back in a few days for the other funeral. When I did go to the grave, I saw that there was a pebble on Kat's grave, and no one had left anything for Alfred. There was nothing there for Alfred, no pebble. Nothing. I called Pam, I was so angry, and said, "You never left a pebble for Alfred." Pam just kept apologizing and apologizing and said she was so sorry, so sorry. Then Tom called me to apologize, and I just said, "You didn't leave a pebble for Alfred." [A pebble is left on a Jewish grave to acknowledge visiting the person's grave.]

Q: What advice would you give to a parent?

A: Make sure you keep the memory alive. Talk about the parent, allowing the parent's memory to be alive even if they are not on this Earth. Allow the child to remember. If the remaining parent should remarry, allow the child to remember their parent that has died. Keep pictures. I was basically not allowed to remember. I was not allowed to remember. My mother was not talked about. It was a subject that was ignored, taboo.

Q: What name would you like us to call you in the book?

A: Maggie. That was the name of my black Lab, who I loved dearly. You will think I'm crazy. She was the best dog. We loved her so much. We had her from the time the kids were two and four years old. She is gone for five years. Her ashes are in our family room. You must think I'm goofy. We tell our golden retriever, "Maggie was the best dog. This interview will keep Maggie's memory alive forever!" [Her attachment to her dog is understandable, given that she acquired her dog when her children were roughly the age she was when her mother became sick and died.]

Q: Maggie is there anything else you would like to add?

A: Jane and Julia think of me as a baby. It drives me crazy. They think I'm still a baby. And I say, "I'm not a baby anymore." Sometimes they still think of me as a baby and forget I'm an adult now, not a baby!

CHAPTER 9

CONSIDERATION FOR INDIVIDUAL THERAPY

Indicators for Individual Therapy

Grief is the normal reaction to the loss of a parent. Bereaved children show a variety of behaviors. Many of the initial behaviors cease without any intervention. The persistence and duration of the mourning process determines whether it is problematic.

The duration and persistence of a symptom can be more significant than the symptom itself. For example, a quiet child may get quieter, an irritable child may have tantrums, a thoughtful child may become withdrawn, and an active child may become hyperactive. It is the duration and persistence that must be noted before help is sought.

Should any of the behaviors on the following list continue for an extended period of time, a professional evaluation should be sought.

- Anxiety—At least six months of excessive worry, fretting, and concern.
- Excessive clinging—The holding on to a person and not wanting, or refusing, to be separated from them for any length of time.
- Fear—Unexplained or excessive or inappropriate fear.
- Crying and sobbing—Unexplainable or inappropriate crying.
- Guilt—Feeling that one is to blame, one has done wrong, one is responsible for something that is in violation of ethical, moral, or religious beliefs.

- Anger and irritability—Excessive outbursts of anger or irritability, either verbal or physical.

- Oppositional behavior—Defiant, disobedient, negative acts; refusing to comply with rules or requests; persistent stubbornness; resistance to directions; testing of limits by ignoring orders; arguing; unwillingness to compromise; deliberately doing things that will annoy other people. This behavior results in impairment in social or academic function.

- Self-esteem problems—Poor self-image, feeling badly about oneself, feelings of inadequacy, doubt.

- Accidents—Unintentional acts that cause injury. For example, falling, tripping, toppling off bikes and skateboards, cutting one's self, burning one's self.

- Agoraphobia—"Anxiety about, or an avoidance of, places or situations from which escape may be difficult or embarrassing."[1]

- Destructive behaviors—Behaviors that cause destruction to objects or people (self or others).

- Vandalism—Damaging behavior such as breaking objects, destroying things, defacing things.

- School difficulties or serious academic reversal—Changes in schoolwork such as poorer grades, unfinished work, incomplete assignments, not doing homework, poorer concentration, forgetfulness, changes in social behavior at school including withdrawn behavior, difficulties with teachers and with peers.

- Difficulties concentrating, preoccupation—Poor concentration and focus, inability to attend, daydreaming.

- Memory difficulties—Forgetfulness, forgetting events and responsibilities (including school assignments, important dates).

- Truancy—Staying away from school or scheduled activities without parental permission.

- School phobia—Refusal or inability to attend school on a regular basis because of pervasive anxiety and physical complaints (headaches, stomach aches).

- Speech problems: Stuttering, mutism—inability to complete words or sentences without halting, repetition of sounds, stammering; a refusal to speak—silence in most interpersonal interactions except for with one or two people.

- Pressured speech—Speech that is relentless, agitated, or overwhelming.
- Reclusiveness—Preference for seclusion or isolation.
- Difficulties making decisions—Inability or reluctance to make choices or judgments.
- Self-isolation—Avoiding being around other people.
- Extreme behavior—Intense or excessive conduct.
- Excessive fighting with others—Unwarranted hostility or struggles with others.
- Bullying behavior—Harassment or hounding of others.
- Lethargy or depressed affect—Apathy, indifference, despondency.
- Panic attacks—Overwhelming anxiety characterized by sweating, trembling, shortness of breath, chest pains, dizziness, nausea, intense fear.
- Feelings of helplessness—Feeling unable to be masterful, successful, or to facilitate change; feeling powerless.
- Running away—Leaving home or school for an extended time.
- Physical ailments—Complaints of headaches, stomach aches, sickness, hurt body parts.
- Lack of interest in previously enjoyed activities—No longer experiencing satisfaction or joy in that which had previously brought pleasure.
- Apathy—Indifference to people, places, or events.
- Lack of emotion/flat affect—No animation, no joy, no anger, no laughter.
- Detachment—Being unaffected by surroundings.
- Inability to relax—Need for constant stimulation, constant activity.
- Rejection of authority.
- Rejection of family or friends—Refusal to interact with family or friends.
- Persistent difficulty talking about the deceased parent—The difficulty can be a refusal to speak about the parent, excessive

tearfulness while talking, or being very abrupt in such conversations.

- Excessive fatigue—Overly tired, listless, and unexplained exhaustion. Little energy.

- Sleeping difficulties (insomnia or hypersomnia)—Insomnia/sleeplessness—There is a difficulty falling asleep and staying asleep. Hypersomnia—There is an excessive sleepiness, and sleep occupies many more hours than usual.

- Persistent nightmares—Occasional nightmares are normal. However, persistent nightmares (sometimes recurring nightmares) are indications of a problem.

- Inability to accept the permanence of the loss—This is a form of denial—a denial that the person will not return.

- Inability to accept parent's absence—See previous condition.

- Excessive distress over separation from home—Unusual anxiety and fear is experienced when the child is separated from home.

- Persistent or excessive worry about loss or about possible harm befalling major attachment figure—This is a common symptom for children who have lost one of their parents. However, when the worry is excessive and starts interfering with the child's daily functioning, help should be sought.

- Persistent or excessive worry of a separation from major loved one—Fears may center on excessive worries about being lost or kidnapped.

- Eating disturbance—Disturbances in the child's routine, normal eating patterns. Sudden and abrupt changes in food preferences or refusal of healthy foods.

- Anorexia/Bulimia—Anorexia is characterized by dramatic weight loss, a refusal to eat a normal amount, an enormous fear of gaining weight, and a distorted perception of the shape or size of the body. For girls, the menstrual cycle is disrupted. Bulimia is characterized by uncontrollable binge-eating followed by an attempt to rid the body of the food consumed, usually through vomiting or the consumption of laxatives and/or excessive exercise or fasting.

- Self-destructive behavior—Behavior in which the individual hurts him- or herself either physically or psychologically.

- Extreme feelings of abandonment or rejection.

- Provoking punishment—Severe feelings of guilt may lead to provocative behavior that will result in punishment.

- Hyperactivity—This may be a manifestation of extreme anxiety following a traumatic event. A determination needs to be made that the hyperactivity is not organically or neurologically based.

- Low energy—A depletion of energy level and activity following the death of a parent is suggestive of depression.

- Persistent reluctance to go to sleep without being near a major attachment figure—Fears and anxieties surrounding the death of a parent can result in children, formerly without many fears, becoming fearful and reluctant to go to sleep alone. Fears about separation, fears about their own deaths, fears about the remaining parent's death, as well as fears about ghosts and nightmares often elicit a reluctance to sleep alone.

- Inability to sleep away from home—This is common in a younger child, especially in the first few weeks and months following a parent's death.

- Phobias—An intense, unreasonable, persistent, excessive fear of certain objects or situations. The fear may be the anticipation of harm from some aspect of the object or situation. The phobic situation is avoided, if possible, or endured while experiencing extreme anxiety.

- Enuresis—Children over the age of five years may regress and wet their beds or clothing when under duress or distress. Enuresis is diagnosed when the behavior occurs several times a week over the course of several (three or four) months. Medical conditions such as diabetes or seizures can result in enuresis.

- Encopresis—Children over the age of four may become fecally incontinent, depositing feces into inappropriate places such as clothes or onto the floor. The behavior occurs at least once a month over the course of several months. Anxiety and/or anger are at the root of this disorder. Medical conditions or medications can result in this symptom.

- Promiscuity—A high frequency of casual, indiscriminate sexual activity with a large number of people.

- Substance abuse (drugs and alcohol)—Drugs and/or alcohol are used to alter mood. Responsibilities at school, home, and work suffer. Hazards include physical danger (for example when driving), disruptions to social and interpersonal relationships. Adolescents are a high-risk group.

- Sociopathic behavior—"A pervasive pattern, or disregard for, and violation of, the rights of others."[2] Repeated deceitfulness, lying, manipulation, stealing, cheating, impulsiveness, aggressiveness, recklessness, irresponsibility, and lack of remorse are characteristic of this disorder.

- Sadism—The infliction of pain or torture or humiliation on people or animals in order to gain pleasure.

- Recklessness—An impulsive disregard for the safety of one's self or others.

- Self-mutilation—Self-injurious acts such as cutting or burning one's self. In a certain type of personality disorder this behavior is often associated with threats of separation or rejection. The self-mutilation can bring relief in that it reaffirms the ability to feel and also allows the individual to make amends for their feeling of being evil. Therapy is strongly indicated whenever self-mutilation occurs.

- Excessive manipulation—Excessive manipulation can be an attempt to control people and situations when the individual feels helpless and out of control. It can also be suggestive of Personality Disorder Syndromes.

- Fire setting—Immediate help should be sought. This symptom is dangerous as well as a cry for help.

- Attention-seeking behavior—This behavior can range from mild (dying hair green, wearing odd/weird clothing) to severe (jumping off a bridge). Behavior that is potentially dangerous.

- Tics—A rapid, recurrent, motoric movement or vocalization, which may worsen when stressed. Examples include eye blinking, coughing, making facial grimaces, jerking of the neck or shoulders, repeated throat clearing, grunting, snorting, making bark-like sounds. More complex tics include jumping, stamping, smelling (an object), using obscene words rapidly and recurrently, repeating one's own sounds or words, imitating someone else's movements. Certain medical conditions or substances can produce tics. The particular tic disorder is diagnosed based on duration and variety of tics and age at onset.

- Excessive masturbation—Recurrent, intense sexual urges that result in excessive self-stimulation with little regard for time, place, or other people.
- Hair-pulling (trichotillomania)—The recurrent pulling out of one's hair, usually resulting in observable hair loss. This is done in a compulsive way.
- Repetitive behaviors (obsessive-compulsive behavior)—Repetitive, compelling impulses to perform acts. There is a preoccupation with perfectionism and control. Examples include hand washing, counting.

How to Find a Therapist

A therapist can be either a psychiatrist, a clinical psychologist, or a social worker.

A psychiatrist is an M.D. who has completed at least four years of specialty training in psychiatry. Often, a psychiatrist is affiliated with a hospital and has admitting privileges. A psychiatrist is the only kind of psychotherapist who can prescribe medication.

A psychologist needs to have either a Ph.D. or an Ed.D. There are different kinds of psychologists, not all of whom receive training in clinical psychotherapy. A clinical psychologist is an individual who has received extensive training in psychotherapy. A clinical psychologist should have completed an internship at an accredited institution and should be licensed by the state.

Social workers are licensed after having completed either an MSW or MS degree or passing a certifying examination. *ACSW* means that the social worker is nationally accredited as a member of the Academy of Certified Social Workers and is qualified to conduct a self-regulated practice by the National Association of Social Workers.

Pastoral counselors are either current or former members of the clergy or individuals with strong religious backgrounds who have entered the counseling field. It is important to ask about their training, since some pastoral counselors are trained in theology, some in counseling, and others in psychotherapy.

A peer counselor is an individual who has no professional training.

Tips on Finding a Good Therapist

1. A personal physician, child's school, church, or psychiatric department of a local hospital can supply an appropriate referral. If possi-

ble, obtain two or three referrals. Talk to each person before deciding where to make a commitment to treatment. How the therapist responds to your concerns should be very helpful in resolving how you feel about working with this person.

2. Typically, your initial contact with a therapist will be over the telephone. If you left a message with a service or on an answering machine, how promptly was your call returned? Did you feel comfortable talking with this person over the phone?

3. Make sure the person is licensed.

4. Make sure the therapist has had training and experience in child therapy.

5. Make sure the therapist has had training and experience in grief therapy.

Important Questions to Ask Any Prospective Therapist

• Is the therapist licensed?

• Has the therapist ever had a license revoked or suspended; has a state or professional ethics board ever disciplined the therapist and would the therapist be willing to discuss it? (You can call the state licensing board to check out his or her license, credentials, and any ethical violations.)

• What kind of training has the individual completed?

• Has the therapist had experience treating children who have experienced loss?

• Is the therapist trained as a child therapist?

• What is the therapist's fee?

• Is there a sliding fee scale?

• Is the therapist qualified to receive medical insurance reimbursement?

• How available will he or she be to you during emergencies over weekends

Resources

Hotlines

The Barr-Harris Children's Grief Center: Institute For Psychoanalysis

(www.barrharris.org)
122 S. Michigan Avenue

Suite 1300, Chicago, IL 80603
1-312-922-7474

The Barr-Harris Children's Grief Center assists bereaved young-sters mourning the death of a parent or sibling. It also helps children who have experienced other losses, such as those occurring in divorce and abandonment. Staff members of the Barr-Harris Center are child psychoanalysts and child psychotherapists with extensive training and experience in treating children.

Bo's Place

(www.bosplace.org)
5601 Austin
P.O. Box 271165
Houston, TX 77277-1185
1-713-942-8339
Fax: 1-713-942-2252

Bo's Place offers programs providing support to children and their families who have experienced the death of a parent or sibling. Bo's Place is founded on the belief that children need to share with other grieving children in order to heal. Bo's Place offers the only ongoing program for grieving children and their families in the Greater Houston Area.

Boy's Town Crisis Hotline

(www.placerteens.org)
1-800-448-3000
Boy's Town National Hotline

This is a 24-hour phone line servicing all young people with any type of problem. Offers advice and referrals.

Center for Loss and Life Transition

(www.counselingforloss.com)
3735 Broken Bow Road
Fort Collins, CO 80525

Over the years, Counseling for Loss has compiled information to help people who have experienced the loss of loved ones. The center compiles letters from children, adolescents, and adults who are griev-ing for loved ones.

Child Abuse Hotline

(www.childhelpusa.org)
1-800-4ACHILD, 1-800-2ACHILD (TDD for Hearing
Impaired)

Child help USA® is one of the largest and oldest national nonprofit organizations dedicated to the treatment and prevention of child abuse and neglect. This organization directly provides help to millions of children and adults whose lives have been traumatized by child abuse.

Civitas Academy

(www.civitas.org)

Using the latest research in early childhood development, Civitas produces and distributes practical, easy-to-use tools that assist adults in making the best possible decisions on behalf of children who are dealing with loss.

Covenant House Hotline

(www.covenanthouse.org)
1-800-999-9999

This hotline offers immediate help to children who feel they have nowhere else to turn.

D'esopo Resource Center

(www.beyondindigo.com)
780 Main Street
Wethersfield, CT 06109
1-860-563-5677

This center offers bereavement education, lectures, and support groups.

The Dougy Center

(www.dougy.org)
P.O. Box 86852
Portland, OR 97288

The Dougy Center was the first center in the United States to provide peer support groups for grieving children. The Dougy Center is a nonprofit organization supported totally by private funds and does not charge a fee for services.

The Dougy Center for Grieving Children provides support to families in Portland and the surrounding region.

Fernside, A Center for Grieving Children

2303 Indian Mound Avenue
Cincinnati, OH 45212
1-513-841-1012

Fernside is a nonprofit, nondenominational organization serving grieving children and their families.

Friends for Survival, Inc.

(www.friendsforsurvival.org)
Suicide Loss Helpline: 1-800-646-7322

Friends For Survival, Inc. is a national nonprofit outreach organization open to those who have lost family or friends to suicide. All staff and volunteers have been directly impacted by a suicide death.

The Good Grief Program

(www.bostonchildhealth.org)
Judge Baker Children's Center
295 Longwood Avenue, Boston, MA 02115
1-617-232-8390

The Good Grief Program provides training, consultation, and crisis intervention in the area of children's bereavement.

Grief Education Institute

2422 South Downing
Denver, CO 80210
1-303-777-9234

The institute offers telephone counseling, educational materials, and a newsletter. The mission of the Institute is to promote optimum support for all bereaved people in order to assist their recovery and prevent chronic illness and ill health.

Grief Recovery Hotline

(www.comnet.org)
1-800-445-4808

This hotline recommends books that deal with grief recovery. Does not offer telephone counseling.

GriefNet

(www.griefnet.org)

GriefNet is an Internet community providing information and communication on all issues related to grief, bereavement, death, dying, physical health, and loss.

Hospice Education Institute

(www.hospiceworld.org)
3 Unity Square
PO Box 98
Machiasport, ME 04655–0098

The Hospice Education Institute serves a wide range of individuals and organizations interested in improving and expanding hospice and palliative care throughout the United States and around the world.

Julie's Place

(www.juliesplace.com)

Julie's Place is a unique web site developed by a young woman who lost her sister in a traumatic event. This site is designed to help siblings deal with traumatic loss.

Kid Save

(www.kidsave.org)
1–800–543–7283

Kid Save attempts to move abandoned and orphaned children expeditiously into permanent and loving families.

Maryland Youth Crisis Hotline

(www.suicidehotlines.com/maryland.html)
1–800–422–0009

This is a suicide and crisis hotline.

Men Against Breast Cancer

(www.menagainstbreastcancer.org).
2379 Lewis Avenue
Rockville, MD 20851-2335
1–301–770–5333

Men Against Breast Cancer (MABC) is the first national, nonprofit organization dedicated to target and mobilize men to be active participants in the fight to eradicate breast cancer.

National AIDS Hotline

(www.ashastd.org/)
1-800-342-AIDS
English: 1-800-342-AIDS
Spanish: 1-800-344-SIDA
Hearing impaired: TDD 1-800-243-7899

The hotline handles about 1 million calls per year from people with questions about prevention, risk, testing, treatment, and other HIV/AIDS-related concerns. Information specialists are available 24 hours a day, 7 days a week, and can answer questions, provide referrals, and send free publications through email.

National Center for Missing and Exploited Children

1-800-843-5678

NCMEC has worked on more than 85,500 cases of missing and exploited children and is recognized as the most effective resource for missing and exploited children.

National Coalition Against Domestic Violence

(www.ncadv.org)
1-800-333-7233

NCADV is dedicated to the empowerment of battered women and their children. Its mission statement explains the organization is committed to the elimination of personal and societal violence in the lives of battered women and their children.

National Domestic Violence Hotline

(www.ndvh.org)
1-800-799-7233

This is a crisis intervention hotline for victims of domestic violence and their concerned family and friends.

National Hospice Organization

(www.nhpco.org)
1901 N. Fort Myer Drive

Arlington, VA 22209
1-703-243-5900

This organization is the oldest and largest nonprofit, public benefit organization devoted exclusively to helping people die with dignity. The organization offers a series of grief guidebooks. It offers services at no charge.

National Runaway and Suicide Hotline

(www.coolnurse.com/hotline.htm)
1-800-621-4000

This national hotline is for runaways and suicide crises.

New England Center for Loss and Transition

(www.neclt.org)
P.O. Box 292
Guilford, CT 06437-0292
1-800-887-5677

Center staff are consultants on children's grief. It offers the largest professional conference on grief and loss in North America.

Parents Anonymous

(www.parentsanonymous.org)
1-800-421-0352

This is a child-abuse prevention organization. Parents Anonymous® Inc. is a community of parents, organizations, and volunteers that are committed to the strengthening of families and the building of strong communities.

Parent Encouragement Center (PEP)

(www.parentencouragement.org)
10100 Connecticut Avenue
Kensington, MD 20895
1-301-929-8824

The goal of this organization is the strengthening of families through education and skill training.

Parents Without Partners

(www.parentswithoutpartners.org)
7910 Woodmont Avenue

Suite 1000
Bethesda, MD 20814
1-800-638-8078

Partners Campaign for Handicapped Children and Youth Closer Look

P.O. Box 1492
Washington, DC 20013
1-202-822-7900

R419 East 86th Street
New York, NY 10028
1-212-876-1590

Ronald McDonald House

(www.rmhc.com)
Ronald McDonald House Charities
One Kroc Drive
Oakbrook, IL 60523
1-630-623-7048

Ronald McDonald Houses are found all over the United States and Canada. They provide a safe, supportive, and caring environment for children and their families in time of crisis.

Sibling Support Center

4800 Sand Point Way, NE
P.O. Box C5371
Seattle, WA 98105
1-206-987-2000

This group offers a support group for young siblings of developmentally disabled children.

Teen Age Grief, Inc.

(www.smartlink.net)
P.O. Box 220034
Newhall, CA 91322-003
1-661-253-1932

This organization offers support and education to young people who are grieving the loss of a loved one. Teen Age Grief, Inc., creates and distributes bereavement guidance programs.

William Wendt Center
(www.charitablechoices.org)
730 Eleventh Street, NW
3rd Floor Washington, DC 20001
1-202-624-0010

This is a center that offers information on grief and bereavement resources.

World Pastoral Center
(www.twpcc.org)
1504 N. Campbell Street
Valparaiso, IN 46385
1-219-531-2230

This support service works in a spiritual way extensively with the bereaved.

Additional Places to Learn about Coping with Grief and Grief Counseling Resources

alt.support.grief (A Grief Support Usenet Newsgroup)

Centre for Grief Education (Australian)

A Place to Honor Grief [Tom Golden]

alt.support.grief Page

Association for Death Education and Counseling

Bereaved Families of Ontario/Metro Toronto

Bereavement and Hospice Support Netline

Bereavement Resources [UK—Legacy, Legal Advice site]

Computerized Aids Ministries

Coping with Unexpected Loss—Judith Gruchawka RN

Crisis, Grief, and Healing: Men and Women (Tom Golden)

Death and Bereavement Links—Growth House

Emotional Support Resources [U Mich]

Grief and Healing Discussion [GAHD]

Grief Link—South Australia (Australian)

Grief Recovery Institute

National Association for Loss and Grief (VIC) (Australian)

Natural Death Centre [London UK]

Pastoral Counseling and Grief Links—Kay's Place

Support for People with Cancer and Caregivers [NIH]

Teenage Grief Inc (TAG)

Thanatolinks: Death Related Web Sites

The Body: A MultiMedia AIDS and HIV Information Resource

The Grieving Process [Against Drunk Drivers]

ZOOM—Bill Chadwick's Page—with Grief Resources

San Francisco: Death links

Places to Learn More about the Way Depression and Suicide Can Affect Our Lives

American Association of Suicidology

Chris Dransfeldt's Suicide Help Page

Depression Hurts, Heals, Inspires

Depression—Patient Guide [AHCPR]

Light For Life Foundation—Suicide Prevention

Panic and Anxiety Page

Prevention Guidelines—Suicide/Homicide (CDC)

TOTT, Turn on to Teens [death, suicide info]

Winter Depression Program Home Page

Appendix: Financial Planning Information

Obviously, the death of a parent can create devastating financial problems. While no guide can replace the kind of in-depth analysis and advice that a good financial advisor provides, many of the principles and guidelines employed by financial advisors can be summarized.

One of the most important steps that a surviving parent can take to stabilize his or her financial situation is to provide a *cash cushion*, which is a pool of money that is readily available to cover emergencies or everyday living expenses should the surviving parent prove unable to work. Many financial advisors recommend a three to six month cash cushion held in checking, savings, and money market funds. By keeping a portion of their funds in relatively liquid assets, the survivor will have the peace of mind that comes with knowing they will be able to pay necessary expenses even if emergencies occur.

A second guideline that parents should follow is making sure that both they and their children are covered by adequate health insurance. While the subject of illness and medical expenses will undoubtedly be painful, it is unlikely to be as painful as the inability to see that a child receives necessary medical attention. By maintaining appropriate levels of medical coverage, a surviving parent can insure against the possibility of one tragedy becoming many.

Thirdly, parents need to make sure that they have insured their ability to earn a living. Most people insure their house and car, but what about the ability to pay for the house and the car? By not having adequate disability insurance protection, parents run the risk of losing their home, savings, and the lifestyle that their children enjoy. While few people like to think about the likelihood of disability, actuaries have shown that almost one person in three is disabled at some point in their careers. Given the additional stress that single parents endure, with the concomitant risk of depression and impaired immune response, disability insurance is even more critical to a surviving parent than therapy. For all but the fortunate few who derive their income mainly from inherited wealth, the continuing ability to earn a living is the most important asset that can be insured, more valuable even than the house or retirement account that were paid for with income that had been earned.

Once the basics have been taken care of, careful attention needs to be given to investments, education planning, tax management, retirement planning, and estate planning.

Many deceased parents will leave behind an estate that needs to be invested. Obviously, investing is best done with the help of a trained professional. However, a consultation with a trained professional is likely to prove less expensive if that professional does not have to educate the surviving parent about the rudiments of finance. To that end, the following are some terms that people will run across when considering investments.

Stock: A stock is a share in a corporation (which is often publicly held). Many stocks are traded daily on an exchange. Ownership of a stock provides the ability to share in any future profits of the underlying corporation. Ownership may also provide the opportunity for capital gains, if the underlying corporation increases in value. Many people believe that over the long term stocks provide the best opportunity to accumulate wealth. This widely held belief should, however, be tempered by the realization that stocks fluctuate in value and may fall in the short term. Whatever the long-term merits of stock, or equity ownership, parents should be aware that for money that may be needed in a relatively short period of time, say less than three years, stocks are usually inappropriate investments.

Bond: A bond represents a corporation's obligation to repay a debt. Government bonds, like the U.S. Treasury bond, represent a government's obligation. While bonds have provided a lower total return than stocks over a long period of time, they are generally believed to be safer than stocks. Bonds are safer because corporations are legally obligated to repay bondholders their interest and principal *before* they pay dividends to stockholders. Consequently, a distressed corporation could have the money to pay its bondholders, but not have the money to provide a dividend to its stockholders.

While bonds are safer than stocks, they do have risks. The two most important risks that investors need to consider are the *default risk* and the *interest rate risk*. The default risk is a risk that the company will not have enough money to pay bondholders their principal. For example, Enron's bondholders lost money when the company declared bankruptcy. A primary interest rate risk is the risk of bondholders receiving less than the original value of their bond. This occurs when interest rates go up and an investor is forced to sell their bond before its expiration date. This could happen because bonds bought on the open market sometimes trade at a price above the amount that the bondholder will receive when the bond matures. When interest rates rise, the prices of bonds fall, so investors who must sell can lose money. Even with these two risks, however, investors who believe they can hold a bond to maturity take less risk than investors who hold a stock in the same corporation for the same amount of time.

Diversification: Once an investor decides which asset class, bonds or stocks, is most appropriate for their risk tolerance and time horizon, they need to understand the benefits of diversification. Even the safest and best companies are risky. The "Widows and orphans stock," AT&T, is trading at a fraction of its all time high; its bonds trade, as of this writing, at a steep discount to the amount they will pay at maturity. If even the bluest of blue chips like IBM and AT&T can prove to be money losers for investors, how can an investor hope to make money? The answer is diversification. By choosing many different stocks or bonds, investors reduce their dependence on the well being of any one corporation. Diversification is Wall Street's way of saying, "Don't put all your eggs in one basket!"

Mutual Funds: Since most individuals don't have enough money to buy a diversified portfolio of bonds or stocks, investment bankers devised the mutual fund. A mutual fund is, as its name suggests, the funds of many people that are pooled together and invested in many different stocks or bonds. Mutual funds are usually bought through a brokerage house, like American Express Financial Advisors or directly from an institution like Vanguard mutual funds.

Annuity: For people who want a guaranteed amount of income each month for the rest of their life, an annuity is often the investment of choice. Annuities are contracts between insurance companies and individuals who provide, in the case of single premium fixed annuities, guaranteed monthly payments for an lump sum up front. While annuities are an effective way of creating a monthly income, they necessarily mean less money for heirs and more money for insurance companies. Still, a surviving parent who needs to pay monthly expenses out of a fixed amount of money from an insurance policy can be certain that they will not outlive their income by buying an insurance policy.

Once the proceeds of an estate are invested, surviving parents need to address both their own financial needs and those of their children. One of the most important things that parents can do for their children is to plan for the child's education. Setting aside money in a tax advantaged plan, such as a 521, will allow the money to grow without being taxed by the federal government.

Once the financial issues relating to their children are taken care of, parents need to deal with their own financial issues. The most immediate issue they will face, from the perspective of financial planning, is tax management. Again the caveat that planning should be done with a professional applies. That said, parents can do many things to proactively reduce their tax burden. The most obvious way to reduce potential tax liabilities is to fully fund retirement accounts (see below) such as 401ks and IRAs. Additionally, parents must itemize and track expenses related to both their business and their children. Finally, for parents who are in the appropriate tax bracket, tax advantaged securities (such as municipal bonds) and shares in limited partnerships which receive tax credits for supplying low income housing may be appropriate investment vehicles.

Even though a surviving parent might feel guilty about preparing for their own retirement in the absence of their spouse, the day will inevitably come when they are unable to continue working. They will either face that day after a lifetime of preparation following a sound retirement plan or they will face it unprepared. Participating fully in a 401k, 403B, or an IRA is a necessary and vital first step. Supplementing their pension savings with additional investments is an excellent idea if it is financially possible. Obviously, the same vehicles that were discussed as possibilities for investing a child's inheritance would be appropriate for investing for retirement; equally obviously, selecting appropriate vehicles is best done with the assistance of a financial planner.

Lastly, and most problematically, surviving parents need to consider their own mortality. While their children will undoubtedly mourn the loss of their sole remaining parent, few children are made better off by the burdens of death taxes and probate. Parents might consider putting some of their money in a trust for their children, purchasing life insurance to pay death taxes, and other estate planning mechanisms to reduce the burdens their children will face when they too die. The simplest, and most important step that a parent can take, is to have a legally valid will that is in the possession of a competent adult.

The authors hope that a few examples will illustrate the principals of financial planning discussed above. Naturally, given that each individual case is different, these examples are provided only to provide a context for how various investment products can be used in a given situation. These examples are *not* intended to be a substitute for the individualized advice of a trained financial professional. Obviously, individuals faced with economic decisions that will affect them and their children for the rest of their lives would be better served by consulting a financial advisor, such as American Express Financial Advisors, Goldman Sachs, Bank Leu, and a registered investment advisor at a local bank or credit union.

The first example is the hypothetical case of a 40-year-old surviving schoolteacher who earns $35,000 per year and has two children, ages 5 and 8. She was left $250,000 in insurance on her husband's death and lives in a $250,000 house with a $150,000 mortgage at 8 percent. When considering her financial options, she first notes that since she spends roughly $2,000 a month, she needs to keep $12,000 in relatively liquid assets, like certificates of deposit, for emergencies. Since she knows that her job will provide health insurance for her family, disability insurance for her, and a death benefit of eight times her salary should she be hit by a bus, she must decide how to invest the $238,000 balance left over after her cash reserve has been set up. Should she pay off her mortgage or should she buy an annuity? Are bonds and stocks appropriate? Would a 521 plan be a luxury she cannot afford or a shrewd decision that will ensure that her children receive the education so important to her and her late husband?

Faced with these daunting decisions, she shrewdly decides to consult with an investment advisor at a well-known firm. The advisor sits down with her, explains his fee, and explains the risks and benefits of several different strategies. After weighing the pros and cons, she realizes that she is unlikely to be able to earn more than 8 percent on her investments given her risk averse nature, so she decides to use $150,000 of her inheritance to pay off her mortgage. She then puts the balance of her money in bond funds since she finds the ups and downs of the stock market unnerving. While she would have liked to have invested money in a 521 plan for her children's education, her financial advisor explained to her that while she can always borrow for her children's education, she cannot borrow for her own retirement—and her 403b is unlikely to provide a sufficient retirement income.

The second hypothetical example is that of a 50-year-old surgeon whose wife, a homemaker, died in a car crash. He earns $300,000 a year, but is responsible for his own health insurance, disability insurance, and life insurance. Since he was already working with a financial professional, he consults his advisor about his options.

The advisor notes that he already has a cash cushion that will pay six months of expenses. Since his wife did not work outside the home, they had failed to insure her life, so no inheritance money will be forthcoming. Unfortunately, since the wife worked extremely hard inside the home, both caring for their retarded daughters and entertaining potential referral sources, the widower will face many new expenses with no additional income or assets. Based on his daughters' likely need to receive care for the rest of their lives and his own need to retire before his hands become arthritic, the surgeon and his advisor decide to modify the surgeon's existing financial plan. They lower his risk tolerance given his new expenses and shift money out of individual stocks and into medium-term corporate bond firms. In addition, having seen the problems caused by a lack of insurance on the deceased wife, the advisor recommends both an increase in the amount of life insurance that the surgeon carries and the establishment of a trust to manage the daughter's inheritance on the surgeon's death. Since the surgeon's referrals will decrease without the wife's entertaining and his expenses will increase because he needs to have a caregiver stay with his daughters while he is at work, the advisor recommends that he move into a smaller home and use the money he saves to buy an annuity. Hopefully, the annuity will cover his new expenses.

A third hypothetical case is that of a 40-year-old widowed store clerk who is raising a 15-year-old son on her own. Her husband died intestate (without a will) and so probate costs and other estate expenses depleted the money from his pension, savings, and the sale of his Harley to $15,000. This money must unfortunately be divided with two children from a previous marriage, so less than $5,000 will be available to help with ongoing expenses. Knowing that she lacks the knowledge and experience to cope with her new situation, the widow speaks to people at a legal clinic, a credit counseling service, and her credit union. All say the same thing: She needs to pay off her existing credit card bills since she is paying 19 percent interest on her balances. She also needs to set up an emergency fund of three months expenses in her checking account. Lastly, she needs to enroll both her son and herself in the health insurance plan at work. While the additional payroll deduction will make life much harder, the terrifying possibility of having to pay for surgery or a hospital stay out of pocket make enrollment in the health insurance plan crucial.

NOTES

Chapter 1

1. Five out of six children will experience the death of a family member. Brooke's Place for Grieving Young People, Inc. (2001).

2. M. H. Nagy, "The Child's Theories Concerning Death," *Journal of Genetic Psychology* 73 (1948): 3–27.

3. M. H. Nagy, "The Child's View of Death," in *The Meaning of Death*, ed. H. Feifel (New York: McGraw-Hill, 1959), 79–98.

4. W. J. Worden, *Children and Grief: When a Parent Dies* (New York: Guilford Press, 1996), 75.

5. P. R. Silverman, S. Nickman, and J. W. Worden, "Detachment Revisited: The Child's Reconstruction of a Dead Parent," *American Journal of Orthopsychiatry* 62 (1992): 494–503.

Chapter 2

1. Thanks to Marsha Huddleston, children's reference librarian at the Harold Washington Library in Chicago, Illinois, from the annotated Mother Goose section, Mother Goose Charms.

When the pilgrims landed in 1666, they had been on the boat for many months. Upon disembarking, the woman immediately began to scrub the grime from their clothes, and so the rhyme was formed.

2. Maurice Sendak, *Where the Wild Things Are* (New York: Harper Collins, 1963).

3. As told to our Motherless Daughters Group, April 1998.

4. These 2 stories (Janet and Ceil) are taken from the Motherless Daughters Group.

Chapter 3

1. S. P. Stuart, review of *The Book of Ruth*, by Hillary Johnson. *New York Times Review*, 26 September 1999, p. 19.

2. As reported in a Motherless Daughters Group, November 1997.

Chapter 4

1. As quoted in J. A. Cutter, "Coming to Terms with Grief After a Longtime Partner Dies," *New York Times*, 13 June 1999, p. 10.

Chapter 5

1. E. O. Wilson, a professor at Harvard, would claim that a step-parenting relationship is inherently difficult because there is rarely a biological relationship between the child and the stepparent. Perhaps his theory of sociobiology explains why Jillian was able to enjoy a harmonious relationship with the aunt who became her stepmother. See also his book, *Sociobiology: The New Synthesis*, 25th anniversary ed. (New Haven, CT: Yale University Press, 1975).

Chapter 6

1. Seven thousand to twelve thousand children in the United States have one parent who commits suicide. Undoubtedly, the number is higher because suicides are underreported. N. B. Webb, ed., *Helping Bereaved Children: A Handbook for Practitioners*, (New York: Guilford Press, 2002), p.137.

2. A. Tan, "Writer's On Writing," *New York Times*, 26 February 2001, p. B2.

3. C. LeDuff, "Living on with a Bitter Fact: 'Yes, Aidan, Daddy is Dead,'" *New York Times*, 11 October 2002, p. A1.

4. C. LeDuff, "A Hard Year without Dad," *New York Times*, 9 August 2002, p. A14.

5. Jonathan Landman, ed., "Portraits of Grief," *New York Times*, 3 October 2001, p. B11.

6. Jonathan Landman, ed., "Portraits of Grief," *New York Times*, 29 December 2001, p. B9.

7. Jonathan Landman, ed., "Portraits of Grief," *New York Times*, 9 March 2002, p. A8.

8. Jonathan Landman, ed., "Portraits of Grief," *New York Times*, October 4, 2001, p. B11.

9. Jonathan Landman, ed., "Portraits of Grief," *New York Times*, November 18, 2001, p. B1.

10. Jonathan Landman, ed., "Portraits of Grief," *New York Times*, November 3, 2001, p. B11.

11. Andrew A. Green, "For Kids, Lost Heroes Also Mom and Dad," http://www.sunspot.net/news (accessed February 20, 2003).

12. Ibid.

Chapter 9

1. American Psychiatric Association, *Diagnostic and Statistical Manual of Mental Disorders*, 4th ed. (Washington, D.C.: American Psychiatric Association, 1994), 665.

2. Ibid.

BIBLIOGRAPHY

Altschul, S. (Ed.). (1988). *Childhood bereavement and its aftermath*. Madison, WI: International Universities Press.

American Psychiatry Association. (1994). *Diagnostic and statistical manual of mental disorders* (4th ed.). Washington, DC: Author.

Anthony, S. (1972). *The discovery of death in childhood and after*. New York: Basic Books.

Arthur, B., & Kemme, M. (1964). Bereavement in childhood. *Journal of Child Psychology and Psychiatry, 5*, 37–49.

Baker, J. E., Sedney, M. A., & Gross, E. (1992). Psychological tasks for bereaved children. *American Journal of Orthopsychiatry, 62*, 105–116.

Balk, D. (1991). Death and adolescents bereavement: Current research and future directions. *Journal of Adolescents Research, 6*, 7–27.

Barnes, M. J. (1964). Reactions to the death of a mother. In R. Eissler, A. Freud, H. Hartmann, & M. Kris (Eds.), *Psychoanalytic study of the child* (Vol. 19, pp. 334–357). New York: International Universities Press.

Beck, A., Sethi, B., & Tuthill, R. (1963). Childhood bereavement and adult depression. *Archives of General Psychiatry, 9*, 295–302.

Bettelheim, B. (1975). *Uses of enchantment: The meaning and importance of fairy tales*. New York: Alfred A. Knopf.

Birtchnell, J. (1972). Early parent death and psychiatric diagnosis. *Social Psychiatry, 7*, 202–210.

Birtchnell, J. (1980). Women whose mothers died in childhood: An outcome study. *Psychological Medicine, 10*, 699–713.

Bowlby, J. (1960). Grief and mourning in infancy and early childhood. *Psychoanalytic Study of the Child, 15*, 9–52.

Bowlby, J. (1961). The Adolf Meyer lecture: Childhood mourning and its implication for psychiatry. *American Journal of Psychiatry, 118,* 481–498.

Bowlby, J. (1978). *Attachment and loss: Attachment* (Vol. 1). London: Penguin Books. (Original work published 1969)

Bowlby, J. (1978). *Attachment and loss: Separation anxiety and anger* (Vol. 2). London: Penguin Books. (Original work published 1973)

Bowlby, J. (1980). *Attachment and loss: Loss, sadness and depression* (Vol. 3). London: The Hogarth Press and the Institute of Psycho-Analysis.

Bowlby, J. (1980). *Loss: Sadness and depression.* New York: Basic Books.

Bowlby, J. (1988). *A secure base: Clinical applications of attachment theory.* London: Routledge.

Bowlby, J. (1990). *Child care and the growth of love.* London: Penguin Books. (Original work published 1953)

Bowlby, J. (1992). *The making & breaking of affectional bonds.* London: Tavistock/Routledge. (Original work published 1979)

Brooke's place for grieving young people, Inc. (2001). Available at http://www.cental-in-chapter-tfc.org/brookesp.html

Brown, G. W., Harris, T. O., & Bifulco, A. (1985). Long-term effects of early loss of a parent. In M. Rutter, C. E. Izald, & P. B. Read (Eds.), *Depression in young people: Developmental and clinical perspectives* (pp. 251–296). New York: Guilford Press.

Cheifetz, P. N., Stavrakakis, G., & Lester, E. P. (1989). Studies of the affective state in bereaved children. *Canadian Journal of Psychiatry, 34,* 688–692.

Crook, T., & Eliot, J. (1980). Parental death during childhood and adult depression: A critical review of the literature. *Psychological Bulletin, 87,* 252–250.

Cutter, J. A. (1999, June 13). Coming to terms with grief after a longtime partner dies. *The New York Times,* p.10.

Deutsch, H. (1937). Absence of grief. *Psychoanalytic Quarterly, 6,* 12–22.

Edelman, H. (1994). *Motherless daughters: The legacy of loss.* Boston: Addison-Wesley Publishing Company.

Erikson, E. (1950). *Childhood and society.* New York: Novton.

Esman, A. (1982). Fathers and adolescent sons. In S. H. Cath, A. R. Gurwitt, & J. M. Ross (Eds.), *Father and child: Development and clinical perspectives.* Boston: Little, Brown and Company.

Fitzgerald, H. (1992). *The grieving child.* New York: Simon & Schuster.

Freud, A., & Burlingham, D. (1943). *War and children.* New York: International Universities Press.

Freud, S. (1955). Mourning and melancholia. In J. Strachey (Ed. and Trans.), *The standard edition of the complete psychological works of Sigmund Freud* (Vol. 14, pp. 243–258). London: Hogarth Press. (Original work published 1923)

Fulton, R. (1967). On death and dying. In E. A. Grollman (Ed.), *Explaining death to children* (pp. 31–47). Boston: Beacon Press.

Furman, E. (1974). *A child's parent dies: Studies in childhood bereavement.* New Haven, CT: Yale University Press.

Furman, E. (1983). Studies in childhood bereavement. *Canadian Journal of Psychiatry, 28*, 241–247.

Furman, E. (1985). Children's patterns in mourning the death of a loved one. In H. Wass and C. A. Corr (Eds.), *Comprehensive pediatric nursing: Childhood and death* (pp. 185–203). Washington, DC: Hemisphere Publishing Corporation.

Furman, R. (1973). A child's capacity for mourning. In E. J. Anthony, and C. Koupenik (Eds.), *Yearbook of the international association for child psychiatry and allied professions: Vol. 2. The child in his family: The impact of disaster and death* (pp. 225–231). New York: Wiley.

Garber, B. (1985). Mourning in adolescence: Normal and pathological. *Adolescent Psychiatry, 12*, 371–387.

Gibala, J. (1999, June 13). Coming to terms with grief after a longtime partner dies. *The New York Times*, p. 10.

Green, Andrew, A. (2003, February) For kids, Lost heroes also mom and dad [23 paragraphs]. Available FTP: Hostname: sunspot.net Directory: www.sunspot.net/news

Greenspan, S. I., & Pollock, G. H. (Eds.). (1980). *The course of life: Psychoanalytic contributions toward understanding personality development* (Vols. 1–3, pp. 659, 550, 608). East Adelphi: Mental Health Study Center, Division of Mental Health Service Programs, National Institute of Mental Health.

Grollman, E. A. (1967). Prologue: Explaining death to children. In E. A. Grollman (Ed.), *Explaining death to children* (pp. 3–27). Boston: Beacon Press.

Grollman, E. A. (1990). *Talking about death.* Boston: Beacon Press.

Grollman, E. A. (Ed.). (1995). *Bereaved children and teens.* Boston: Beacon Press, 1995.

Harris, M. (1995). *The loss that is forever: The lifelong impact of the early death of a mother or father.* New York: Penguin Books.

Hrdy, S. B. (1999). *Mother nature: A history of mothers, infants, and natural selection.* New York: Pantheon Books.

Kubler-Ross, E. (1969). *On Death and Dying.* New York: Macmillan.

Landman, Jonathan. (Ed.). (2001, October 3). Portrait of grief. *The New York Times*, p. B11.

Landman, Jonathan. (Ed.). (2001, October 4). Portrait of grief. *The New York Times*, p. B11.

Landman, Jonathan. (Ed.). (2001, November 3). Portrait of grief. *The New York Times*, p. B11.

Landman, Jonathan. (Ed.). (2001, November 18). Portraits of grief. *The New York Times*, p. B11.

Landman, Jonathan. (Ed.). (2002, March 9). Portrait of grief. *The New York Times*, p. A8.

LeDuff, C. (2002, August 9). A hard year without dad. *The New York Times*, p. A14.

LeDuff, C. (2002, October 11). Living on with a bitter fact: "Yes, Aidan, daddy is dead." *The New York Times*, p. A1.

Lifton, R. J. (1995). *The broken connection: On death and the continuity of life.* New York: Basic Books.

Mahler, M. S. (1950). *Helping children to accept death.* New York: Child Association of America.

Mahler, M. S. (1961). On sadness and grief in infancy and childhood. *Psychoanalytic Study of the Child, 16,* 337–351.

Mahler, M. S., Pine, F., & Bergman, A. (1975). *The psychological birth of the human infant: Symbiosis and individuation.* London: Hutchinson.

Miller, J. B. M. (1971). Children's reactions to the death of a parent: A review of psychoanalytic literature. *Journal of the American Psychoanalytic Association, 19,* 697–719.

Nagy, M. H. (1948). The child's theories concerning death. *Journal of Genetic Psychology, 73,* 3–27.

Nagy, M. H. (1959). The child's view of death. In H. Feifel (Ed.), *The Meaning of Death* (pp. 79–98). New York: McGraw-Hill.

Offer, D., Ostrov, E., & Howard, K. I. (1981). *The adolescent: A psychological self portrait.* New York: Basic Books.

Oltjenbruns, K. A. (2001). Developmental context of childhood: Grief and regrief phenomena. In M. S. Stroebe, R. O. Hansson, & H. Schut (Eds.), *Handbook of bereavement research: consequences, coping and care* (pp. 169–198). Washington, DC: American Psychological Association.

Piaget, J. (1955). *The construction of reality in the child.* New York: Basic Books.

Piaget, J. (1981). *Death and the family: The importance of mourning.* London & Boston: Faber & Faber. (Original work published 1974)

Raphael, B. (1982). The young child and the death of a parent. In C. M. Parkes and J. Stevenson-Hindes (Eds.), *The place of attachment in human behavior* (pp. 131–150). New York: Basic Books.

Rubel, B. (2000). *But I didn't say goodbye.* New Jersey: Griefwork Center, Inc.

Sachs, H. (1942). Beauty life and death. In A. A. Roback (Ed.), *The creative unconscious* (pp. 147–240). Cambridge, MA: Science Art Publishers.

Sendak, M. (1963). *Where the wild things are.* New York: Harper Collins.

Shaver, P. R., & Tancredy, C. M. (2001). Emotion, attachment and bereavement: A conceptual commentary. In M. S. Strobe, R. O. Hansson, W. Stroebe, & H. Schut (Eds.), *Handbook of bereavement research: Consequences, coping, and care* (pp. 63–88). Washington, DC: American Psychological Association.

Shneidman, E. S. (1995). *The psychology of suicide: A clinician's guide to evaluation and treatment* (Rev. ed.). Northvale, NJ: Jason Aronson.

Silverman, P. R., Nickman, S., & Worden, J. W. (1992). Detachment revisited: The child's reconstruction of a dead parent. *American Journal of Orthopsychiatry, 62,* 494–503.

Strobe, M. S., & Schut, H. (2001). Models of coping and bereavement: A review. In M. S. Strobe, R. O. Hansson, W. Stroebe, & H. Schut (Eds.),

Handbook of bereavement research (pp. 375–403). Washington, DC: American Psychological Association.

Strobe, M. S., Hansson, R. O., Stroebe, W., & Schut, H. (Eds.). (2001). *Handbook of bereavement research.* Washington, DC: American Psychological Association.

Stroebe, M. S., Stroebe, W., & Hansson, R. O. (1997). *Handbook of bereavement: Theory, research and intervention.* London: Cambridge University Press.

Stuart, S. P. (1999, September 26). *The book of Ruth. The New York Times Book Review*, p. 19.

Tan, A. (2001, February 26). Writer's on writing. *New York Times*, p. B2.

Webb, N. B. (Ed). (2002). *Helping bereaved children: A handbook for practitioners.* New York: Guiliford Press.

Wilson, E. O. (1975). *Sociobiology: The new synthesis* (25th Anniversary ed.). New Haven, CT: Yalem University Press.

Winnicott, D. W. (1953). Transitional objects and transitional phenomena. *International Journal of Psycho-Analysis, 34,* 89–97.

Worden, J. W. (1991). *Grief counseling and grief therapy* (2nd ed.). New York: Springer.

Worden, J. W. (1996). *Children and grief: When a parent dies.* New York: Guilford Press.

INDEX

About the Series Editor
and Advisory Board

CHRIS E. STOUT, Ph.D., MBA, holds a joint governmental and academic appointment in Northwestern University Medical School, and serves as Illinois's first chief of psychological services. He served as an NGO special representative to the United Nations, was appointed by the U.S. Department of Commerce as a Baldridge examiner, and served as an advisor to the White House to both political parties. He was appointed to the World Economic Forum's Global Leaders of Tomorrow. He has published and presented more than 300 papers and 22 books. His works have been translated into five languages. He has lectured across the nation and internationally in 16 countries, visiting more than 50 nations. He has been on missions around the world and has summated three of the World's Seven Summits. He is past president of the Illinois Psychological Association and is a member of the National Academy of Practice. He has been widely interviewed by media, including CNBC, CNN, the Oprah Winfrey Show, *Time*, *Chicago Tribune*, and *The Wall Street Journal*. His work was recognized by the Senate and House with the proclamation of "Dr. Chris E. Stout Week."

BRUCE E. BONECUTTER, Ph.D., is director of behavioral services at the Elgin Community Mental Health Center, the Illinois Department of Human Services state hospital serving adults in greater Chicago. He is also a clinical assistant professor of psychology at the University of Illinois at Chicago. A clinical psychologist specializing in health, consulting, and forensic psychology, Mr. Bonecutter is also a longtime member of the American Psychological Association Taskforce on Children and the Family. He is a member of organizations including the Association for the Treatment of Sexual Abusers, International, the Alliance for the Mentally Ill and the Mental Health Association of Illinois.

JOSEPH A. FLAHERTY, M.D., is chief of psychiatry at the University of Illinois Hospital, a professor of psychiatry at the University of Illinois College of Medicine and a Professor of Community Health Science at the UIC College of Public Health. He is a founding member of the Society for the Study of Culture and Psychiatry. Dr. Flaherty has been a consultant to the World Health Organization, to the National Institutes of Mental Health, and also to the Falk Institute in Jerusalem. He has been the director of undergraduate and graduate education in the Department of Psychiatry at the University of Illinois. Dr. Flaherty has also been staff psychiatrist and chief of psychiatry at Veterans Administration West Side Hospital in Chicago.

MICHAEL HOROWITZ, Ph.D., is president and professor of clinical psychology at the Chicago School of Professional Psychology, one of the nation's leading not-for-profit graduate schools of psychology. Earlier, he served as dean and professor of the Arizona School of Professional Psychology. A clinical psychologist practicing independently since 1987, his work has focused on psychoanalysis, intensive individual therapy and couples therapy. He has provided disaster mental health services to the American Red Cross. Mr. Horowitz's special interests include the study of fatherhood.

SHELDON I. MILLER, M.D., is a professor of psychiatry at Northwestern University, and director of the Stone Institute of Psychiatry at Northwestern Memorial Hospital. He is also director of the American Board of Psychiatry and Neurology, director of the American Board of Emergency Medicine and director of the Accreditation Council for Graduate Medical Education. Dr. Miller also an examiner for the American Board of Psychiatry and Neurology. He is founding editor of the American Journal of Addictions, and founding chairman of the American Psychiatric Association's Committee on Alcoholism. He is a member and past president of the executive committee for the American Academy of Psychiatrists in Alcoholism and Addictions.

DENNIS P. MORRISON, Ph.D., is chief executive officer at the Center for Behavioral Health in Indiana, the first behavioral health company ever to win the JCAHO Codman Award for excellence in the use of outcomes management to achieve healthcare quality improvement. He is president of the board of directors for the Community Healthcare Foundation in Bloomington, and has been a member of the board of directors for the American College of Sports Psychology. He has served as a consultant to agencies including the Ohio Department of Mental Health, Tennessee Association of Mental Health Organizations, Oklahoma Psychological Association, the North Carolina Council of Community Mental Health Centers and the National Center for Heath Promotion in Michigan. Dr. Morrison served across 10 years as a medical service corporal officer in the U.S. Navy.

WILLIAM H. REED, M.D., is a clinical and forensic psychiatrist, and consultant to attorneys and courts throughout the United States. He is clinical professor of psychiatry at the University of Texas Health Science Center. Dr. Reed is also an adjunct Professor of psychiatry at Texas A&M College of Medicine and Texas Tech University School of Medicine, as well as a clinical faculty member at the Austin Psychiatry Residency Program. He is chairman of the Scientific Advisory Board and medical examiner to the Texas Depressive & Manic-Depressive Association, as well as an examiner for the American Board of Psychiatry & Neurology. He has served as president of the American Academy of Psychiatry and the Law, as chairman of the Research Section for an International Conference on the Psychiatric Aspects of Terrorism, and as medical director for the Texas Department of Mental Health and Mental Retardation. Dr. Reid earned an Exemplary Psychiatrist Award from the National Alliance for the Mentally Ill. He has been cited on the Best Doctors in America listing since 1998.

About the Authors

PADDY GREENWALL LEWIS, Ph.D., has been a clinical psychologist in private practice for more than 25 years. She specializes in child psychology. She developed and has run groups for motherless daughters. Lewis trained under and worked for Bruno Bettelheim at the University of Chicago Orthogenic School, and later spent 10 years as Chief Psychologist at the Siegel Institute at Michael Reese Hospital and Medical Center.

JESSICA G. LIPPMAN, Ph.D., is a clinical psychologist who has been in practice in the Chicago area for 25 years. She specializes in child psychology and regularly treats children and youths who have lost a parent. With Dr. Lewis, she developed a group for motherless daughters. She is an instructor in Clinical Psychology and Behavioral Sciences at Northwestern University Medical School. Previously, she served as Chief Psychologist at the Siegel Institute at Michael Reese Hospital.